Children in Jericho, Vermont, play among fallen leaves.

NEW ENGLAND

Prepared by the Special Publications Division, National Geographic Society, Washington, D.C.

Land of Scenic Splendor

Lobster boats ride quietly at anchor in Bass Harbor at the southern tip of Maine's Mount Desert Island.

NEW ENGLAND:
Land of Scenic Splendor

Contributing Authors: Tor Eigeland,
    Christine Eckstrom Lee, Jane R. McCauley,
    Tom Melham, Cynthia Russ Ramsay
Contributing Photographers: Tor Eigeland,
    Nicholas DeVore III, Sarah Leen,
    Michael Melford, Philip Schermeister

Published by The National Geographic Society
Gilbert M. Grosvenor, *President and Chairman of the Board*
Melvin M. Payne, Thomas W. McKnew, *Chairmen Emeritus*
Owen R. Anderson, *Executive Vice President*
Robert L. Breeden, *Senior Vice President, Publications and
    Educational Media*

Prepared by The Special Publications Division
Donald J. Crump, *Director*
Philip B. Silcott, *Associate Director*
Bonnie S. Lawrence, *Assistant Director*

Staff for this book
Ron Fisher, *Managing Editor*
Charles E. Herron, *Illustrations Editor*
Joseph A. Taney, *Art Director*
Jody Bolt, *Consulting Art Director*
Patricia F. Frakes, *Senior Researcher*
Barbara Bricks, Monique F. Einhorn, *Researchers*
Leslie Allen, Richard M. Crum,
    Christine Eckstrom Lee, Jane R. McCauley,
    Cynthia Russ Ramsay, *Picture Legend Writers*
John D. Garst, Jr., Judith F. Bell, Susan I. Friedman,
    Map Research
Sandra F. Lotterman, *Editorial Assistant*
Artemis S. Lampathakis, *Illustrations Assistant*

Engraving, Printing, and Product Manufacture
George V. White, *Director,* and
Vincent P. Ryan, *Manager,*
   Manufacturing and Quality Management
David V. Showers, *Production Manager*
Kevin Heubusch, *Production Project Manager*
Lewis R. Bassford, *Assistant Production Manager*
Kathie Cirucci, Timothy H. Ewing,
   Senior Production Assistants
Carol R. Curtis, *Senior Production Staff Assistant*

Susan A. Bender, Catherine G. Cruz, Marisa Farabelli,
   Karen Katz, Lisa A. LaFuria, Eliza Morton,
   Dru Stancampiano, *Staff Assistants*

Lucinda L. Smith, *Indexer*

Autumn paints New England hillsides and pastures with swaths of subdued colors. Darkening skies here threaten a farm near Washington, Vermont.

CONTENTS

Evening lights glitter across Boston, the

commercial and educational hub of New England. Faneuil Hall anchors a harbor-side marketplace.

Boxed in by New York, Canada, and the Atlantic Ocean, New England makes up in spirit what it lacks in size. From the days of the Pilgrims through revolutions in politics and industry to today's crowds of tourists and exurbanites, the six states—Maine, New Hampshire, Vermont, Massachusetts, Rhode Island, Connecticut—have remained a single distinctive "place" in the American mind.

NEW ENGLAND

Saint John
Allagash
Allagash Falls
Presque Isle
Churchill L.
CANADA
UNITED STATES
Katahdin 5,267 ft.
Stacyville
Moosehead Lake
St. Croix R.
Penobscot
Passamaquoddy Indian Township
MAINE
Big Lake
Cobscook Bay
Lubec
Cutler
Beals I.

CANADA
UNITED STATES
Colebrook
Upper Ammonoosuc R.
Lake Champlain
Mt. Mansfield 4,393 ft.
Sheffield
Grafton Notch
Monroe
Burlington
Stowe
Danville
Mt. Washington 6,288 ft.
Augusta
Cadillac Mt. 1,530 ft.
South Woodbury
Peacham
Pittston
Camden
Mount Desert I.
Montpelier
Crawford Notch
Sabbathday Lake
Rockport
Bass Harbor
Adirondack Mountains
VERMONT
White Mts.
Fryeburg
Wiscasset
Orford
Saco
Boothbay Harbor
Champlain Canal
Woodstock
NEW HAMPSHIRE
Portland
Casco Bay
Monhegan I.
Plymouth
Green Mountains
Connecticut
Canterbury
Kennebunkport
NEW YORK
Concord
Merrimack R.
Manchester
Portsmouth
Exeter
Peterborough
Mt. Greylock 3,491 ft.
Greenville
Cape Ann
Lowell
Marblehead
Salem
Berkshire Hills
Stockbridge
Barre
Concord
Walden Pond
Lexington
Stellwagen Bank
Bashbish Falls
MASSACHUSETTS
Boston
Dedham
Quincy
Bartholomew's Cobble
Plymouth
Provincetown
Highland Light
Long Pt.
Pawtucket
Kent
Cornwall
Hartford
Providence
Cape Cod
CONNECTICUT
RHODE ISLAND
New Bedford
Harwich Port
Housatonic
East Haddam
New London
Adamsville
Woods Hole
Georges Bank
Hudson
New Haven
Mystic Seaport
Newport
Byram
Long Island Sound
Martha's Vineyard
Nantucket I.
New York

Atlantic Ocean

0   50   100 MI
0   50   100 KM

FOREWORD

By Dr. Robert C. Seamans, Jr.
Board of Trustees, National Geographic Society

I grew up in Salem, Massachusetts, within ten blocks of the House of the Seven Gables. Our home, built in the 17th century, had low ceilings with exposed oak beams that were a continual hazard for my 6-foot 4-inch father. Although my family were interested in historical preservation, my grandmother viewed the witch trials as a disgrace and felt that all evidence from that hysterical period should be downplayed or destroyed.

This heritage didn't bother my friends or me as we walked past the Witch House and played baseball at a park in the shadow of Gallows Hill. On rainy Saturdays, we often were encouraged to visit the Peabody Museum, in front of which stands a large, old-fashioned iron anchor. Once inside, we could view souvenirs from the China trade. There were models of fully rigged clipper ships, ivory artifacts carved by skilled sailors, some so small they had to be viewed through a magnifying glass, and mysterious Oriental robes of brightly colored silks.

Anyone whose home is in New England will find, as I have, much that is familiar in *New England: Land of Scenic Splendor*. The book must have been a challenge for its authors and photographers, because New England has a wide variety of resources, in marked contrast to its small size. Rocky coasts, sandy beaches, forests and lakes, navigable rivers, rolling farmland and vibrant cities, hills and mountains—all can be found within New England's borders. And many of its cultural and educational institutions are famed around the world.

Over the past seven decades I've witnessed change on many fronts. In my early years, toe straps bound me to my heavy wooden skis. Later, when I entered the Vermont Downhill on Mount Mansfield, there were no tows to take me to the top of the Nose Dive for the start of the race. (I was last in a freezing mist!) Today more than 70 ski areas in New England report daily on the conditions of their slopes, all serviced by modern lifts.

The Custom House Tower, which used to be the best observatory for a view of Boston and its surroundings, is now lost in a forest of taller buildings. New England's venture capital and intellectual richness have provided the basis for many new companies. Some are housed in old textile mills, some in local garages, and some in industrial parks. Cultural organizations have increased in number, and their facilities have been refurbished. Community colleges and state universities now supplement the great number of private educational institutions.

Marblehead has grown dramatically, with moorings for some 2,500 boats, but it is still governed by taxpayers voting at town meetings. Those attending, however, are considered to be "foreigners" by the native dwellers unless they are second-generation inhabitants. Native New Englanders who read this book will see themselves mirrored in many dimensions, and outsiders will better understand how and why the natives live here, in spite of the chill winds, fog, ice, and snow. For as the readers of this book will discover, there are as many splendid facets to life in New England as there are changes in its uncertain weather.

I

THE ROOTS OF NEW ENGLAND

By Christine Eckstrom Lee   *Photographs by Sarah Leen*

A land long lived-in sings with many voices. There are faraway murmurings from times before time in the tongues of people who first tracked the soil, and voices, strange to us now, that speak from the pages of old leather volumes, words of explorers and missionaries and the soldiers of kings. There are the collected voices of history books, and there are the voices of another history, held in each individual memory: the old silver bowl in the cabinet that carries a family tale; the generations of community remembrances released by the singing of a hymn; the world imagined through an ancestor's spectacles; the story whispered to a grandchild, now old enough to know.

In New England, stony and seabound and long lived-in, I journeyed through seasons and landscapes like a time traveler, to

Christmas-card towns huddled around village greens and cities that rise around the graves of patriots, to the dark forests the Indians knew and the shores where they paused, watching sails grow larger on the eastern horizon.

In the region that 17th-century English explorers called New England—as other European powers had claimed vast territories to the north and south as New France and New Spain—I considered the rich tapestry of events and peoples that have shaped its history: the heritage of Native Americans, the role of religious communities, the Revolutionary War, the seafaring

New England's seaborne heritage finds expression in a model ship (above) and in Massachusetts' Plymouth Rock, where legend has it that the Pilgrims landed in 1620.

traditions that expanded our national horizons, and the industrial revolution that led us to fashion a new destiny on our own home ground.

I sought out the places of our history books, and found people whose families and lives speak both to New England's past and to the other history—of memories, myths, and tales passed along—that, as much as what is in the books, makes us who we are.

A New Englander once told his son, "With a poet in your pocket, you will never be alone," and I appreciated that advice as I traveled, accompanied by a copy of Henry Wadsworth Longfellow's works. New England's 19th-century poet laureate, who spun history into lilting, toe-tapping verse, has given us national myths and folk heroes: Hiawatha, Miles Standish, Paul Revere, Evangeline. Longfellow lines memorized in my youth became a refrain for New England's history and for the blend of fact and lore that has more truth and wisdom than either one alone.

A rchly the maiden smiled, and, with eyes
overrunning with laughter,
Said, in a tremulous voice,
'Why don't you speak for yourself, John?'
—The Courtship of Miles Standish

John Alden, the *Mayflower* Pilgrim whose roundabout betrothal to Priscilla Mullens was celebrated by Longfellow, was himself an ancestor of the poet, and even Priscilla's famous query was handed down to Longfellow as a family tradition.

Whatever the truth of the story, Plymouth and the Pilgrims are ingrained in the American consciousness, and although historians have challenged our folk images of Plymouth Rock and the nature of the Pilgrim experience the myth continues, with

its message of hardships endured for an ideal revered.

I stopped to see Plymouth Rock on a cold and gray October day. A granite portico, like a temple, shelters it by the shore of Plymouth Harbor. The sea laps close, ducks swim by, and boats bob in the water beyond, halyards clinking. No one else was visiting the rock just then, but the strength of its legend found expression in the dozens of pennies tossed around it, rings of silent wishes.

The Pilgrims may be seen as the first among many who viewed the New World as a fresh map, a place to fashion a life not possible in the land they left behind. From the mid-18th to the mid-19th centuries, scores of religious and utopian communities sprang up across America, and many had their origins in the Northeast. Most were short-lived, but in the rolling lake country of western Maine I visited one such religious community that, although now small in numbers, has survived there for more than two centuries.

The eight Shakers of Sabbathday Lake are the last of their sect still practicing their faith and way of life as an active community. Celibate and pacifist, Shakers are Christians who hold goods in common and, in addition to the Bible, revere the teachings of their founder, Ann Lee, known as Mother Ann.

"I don't think new members will ever flock to this community the way they used to," said Sister Frances Carr, "but I do think that it's very important for people to know that Shakerism is alive and well."

I met Sister Frances at the Sabbathday Lake dwelling house, a large brick home set amid a clutch of clean white clapboard buildings—offices, workshops and barns, the meetinghouse, library, museum, and

store—grouped along both sides of a rural route known locally as Shaker Road. Sister Frances, the kitchen deaconess, orchestrated the preparation of the noontime meal as we talked in the kitchen, hub of the house and a changing stage of activity. Sister Minnie peeled potatoes; Sister Marie made apple pies; Sister Mildred rushed off to tend the shop; Sister Meg called from Portland—did anyone need anything from town? Brother Wayne passed through on his way to the barn; Brother Arnold brought fresh tomatoes from the garden; and Sister Frances, reaching into a roaster pan full of chicken, her hands flecked with tarragon, exclaimed, "Ah, summertime, and the living is easy!"

In New England—and Maine especially—the season of easy living is brief. "Climate and geography cannot help but make you," Sister Frances said, "and it has made New Englanders tough. I feel that hardship has helped us grow stronger spiritually. It's in New England that Shaker communities have lasted the longest, and ours was always the poorest. We were known as 'the least of Mother's children in the East,' but here we are, still here."

Shaker life today is a sensible and surprising mix of traditions kept and changes embraced. All the women wore running shoes. "They're more comfortable," said Sister Frances. The kitchen wall had two telephones, side by side: one modern, to the outside world; one hand-cranked, to connect community buildings. "It saves steps," said Sister Marie. "We used to have a wood stove," said Sister Frances, "but we've had gas now for 25 years, and it's great. Some people talk about the good old days—they can have them!"

The Shakers are famous for the exquisite design and craftsmanship of their furniture, as well as for a volume of inventions far out of proportion to their numbers: washing machines, circular saws, swivel feet for chairs, flat brooms, clothespins, water-repellent cloth. Efficiency, simplicity, and the aim for perfection, as expressed in their many labor-saving improvements and clean, minimal designs, were part of the faith, as reflected in an admonition to "put your hands to work and your hearts to God." Sister Mildred said, "There's religion in every one of those chairs."

"We're human beings, we're not perfect, but striving for perfection is our daily labor, for the love of God," Sister Frances said. "And if we in this community can live up to what we are professing, maybe our example will be a little candle in the night."

On Sunday I joined the Shakers at their worship meeting, where guests are welcome. Men and women, including seven visitors, sat in separate pews, facing one another during a service of scripture readings, spontaneous songs, pauses for prayer, and plain-spoken thoughts from different members and visitors.

The Shakers are guided by the light of those who have gone before them. They think of all Shakers, past and present, as family, and address one another as brother and sister. Around the walls of the dwelling house are portraits of Shakers who were known to at least one member of the community, like paintings of ancestors. Eldress Prudence Stickney took young Sister Frances under her wing, showing her how to make dishes that had been prepared by generations of Shaker cooks; Eldress Harriet Coolbroth carried the gift of a repertoire of songs dating back to Shaker beginnings and taught them to Sister Mildred. In Sunday meeting, when Sister Mildred leads the beautiful Shaker melody, "Simple Gifts," a symphony of voices would sing with her.

*S*till stands the forest primeval;
but under the shade of its branches
Dwells another race,
with other customs and language.
— *Evangeline*

Across the Bay of Fundy from *Evangeline*'s Acadia, the wild forests and river lands of easternmost Maine are the traditional home of the Passamaquoddy Indians. Together with their neighbors, the Maliseet, they were known to other tribes as Wabanaki, "People of the Dawn," and as with most Native Americans, the Passamaquoddy have carried their history through oral traditions, passing down the words of the ancestors to each generation.

"My grandmother brought me up on the legends of our people as our history," said Wayne Newell, a tribal leader and teacher, "and in time you come to realize that they're not just fables and stories of animals; they are lessons for community living, grounded in something real. They carry powerful messages and values. They tell you who you are."

I met Wayne at the Passamaquoddy School in Indian Township, Maine, on a morning made for myths. The day before, the forests were hot with fall colors; from the crest of a hill the land looked like a vast bed of glowing coals, and the waters of Big Lake, where Indian Township lies, danced in the wind, blueberry-blue in the sun.

Then in the night the first frost came, glazing the world white. Just after sunrise Big Lake puffed huge clouds of fog, as if it were steaming, and every twig of every tree twinkled with rime. As Wayne and I talked at the school, we glanced out the window now and then, watching the land change, as the sun's warmth melted the frost, and the leaves dripped, turning red and gold again.

"This weather means that the loons will start leaving for the coast," said Wayne. Maine's North Woods are the country of the loon, the bird with the cry like haunted laughter that echoes far over the waters. "There are many legends about the loon," Wayne told me. "They are messengers and watchdogs. They call across the lakes, deeper and deeper into the woods, sending messages to Koluskap."

Koluskap is the central figure of Passamaquoddy legends. Like the coyote and the raven in tribal legends of the Great Plains and the West, Koluskap is both a hero and a trickster; he has great power and can assume many forms, but overall he is good, a helper to the people. The legends about him reveal an ancestral view of the relationship between man and nature, wrapped around a small nugget of wisdom for life.

Wayne has played many roles in his 47 years, most of them directed toward preserving Passamaquoddy culture. He has worked in television and radio and in tribal planning and health services; he received a master's degree from Harvard and a Ford Foundation Fellowship; he was an Indian rights activist and then served on several commissions on Indian affairs; he was appointed by President Carter to the National Advisory Council on Indian Education; he has recorded Passamaquoddy oral histories, helped to translate their language from oral to written form, and set up the first bilingual education program at the elementary school. He is also a tribal musician. "My first love," said Wayne.

His heightened appreciation of music and the sound of words are balanced, as Wayne says, by a visual handicap. He sees weakly through thick glasses that greatly magnify his eyes, as if in demonstration of a larger vision. "Legally I'm blind," he told me. "But I operated a television camera for three years!" He laughed. "I just figured out a way to do it."

If storytelling holds the messages of Passamaquoddy culture, language is the code and the key to continuing tribal heritage. "We were lucky," said Wayne. "Unlike other tribes, we have survived with our language intact, and part of that has been due to mother nature's isolation. But in recent years, with fewer young people speaking the language, and with the impact of television especially, Passamaquoddy was in danger of becoming a graveyard language. We might have lost our oral tradition forever."

Wayne helped prepare the first Passamaquoddy dictionary and schoolbooks. "I learned how difficult it is to translate an oral language into a written one," he said. "So much is in the gestures and inflections. But it was fascinating to see into the words and trace their origins."

In Passamaquoddy, the word for telephone — *mah-te-kde-mu-wa-gyn* — means, roughly, "the line that jingles at the end." "The word is onomatopoeic," said Wayne, "and you know it has to do with a string, like a fishing line, by the way it is constructed. There are two concepts in the word: the sound and something that's strung."

Nearly four centuries ago, a Passamaquoddy word came into use that would be spoken more and more as time passed. *Wanooch* is a term for white people. "It doesn't really translate as 'white person,'" Wayne explained. "Literally, it means, 'From whence did they come?'"

Wanooch was probably first uttered with that meaning in 1604 from the forested banks of the St. Croix River, along what is now the U.S.–Canada border. In that year, more than a decade before the *Mayflower* set sail, a group of Frenchmen that included the explorer Champlain attempted to settle on a tiny island in the river. I had seen it from the shore, a rocky mound of perhaps five acres in the center of a wide, swift river. To choose such a place, they must have been scared.

"And we were in the woods, watching, thinking, 'Who are these crazy people?'" said Wayne. After a bitter winter, during which nearly half the men died, the French abandoned the site—but not their settlement efforts—and since 1604 Passamaquoddy land has been a border: between France and England, between the British and the Americans, now between Canada and the United States.

Several years ago Wayne worked with a team to prepare a Passamaquoddy account of the Revolutionary War for the school. It includes the story of a Passamaquoddy, Chief Francis Joseph Neptune. At the British siege of Machias in 1777—a turning-point battle for Maine—he fired a single

*Wielding cans like these, workers oiled
the wheels of industries that flourished
throughout 19th-century New England.*

shot from a great distance that felled an officer of the British fleet. The ensuing battle caused the ships to retreat, never to return. The Passamaquoddy still have a letter from George Washington thanking them for their assistance during the war.

In 1980, when the United States settled a long-fought land claim with the Passamaquoddy, Wayne Newell discovered to his surprise that he was a direct descendant of the last hereditary chief. Francis Joseph Neptune, and generations of chiefs before him, are Wayne's own ancestors.

"I only knew that I was a member of that family," said Wayne, "and that I was a descendant of Lewis Mitchell, who was an Indian rights advocate a century ago. We've all read his famous speech to the Maine legislature, about the men who have grown rich from the timber of Passamaquoddy land. It almost takes you back to—today.

"But America is our common ground now," he added. "We live with two cultures; it's a balancing act. What do we give our children? I tell people that our spirits have borne us through all of this, and I believe that it is through our heritage that we're going to find an answer."

Wayne often goes off in his boat alone, or to the solitude of the forest, to think. "When I'm out in the woods, I feel close to my creator. I feel connected to something more powerful than me," he said. "I think that the pursuit of tradition, symbolism, ceremony, some agreed-to order, are all important in finding self. And if you do find a part of the peace we all search for, you have a responsibility to pass that on to the next generation."

I had read of a legend about Koluskap, that he had grown disappointed with the people's way of living and had decided to leave the earth, paddling off in a great canoe. After he disappeared from sight, suddenly all the creatures of the earth could no longer understand one another. Before, they shared a common language, and now they were frightened and lonely and hoped Koluskap would return.

"He didn't physically leave the earth," Wayne explained. "He just went way back in the woods. For you to find him you have to go through a long, hard journey. He invites you to find him, but it will not be easy. There's a real message in his saying, 'I am still here,'" Wayne reflected. "Koluskap says, 'You can seek me out.' It's a real nice thing to know."

I remember the black wharves and the slips,
  And the sea-tides tossing free . . .
  And the beauty and mystery of the ships,
And the magic of the sea.
                    —*My Lost Youth*

His mother cried when Jose Ramos kissed her goodbye in April 1921. A long and terrible drought had devastated their home in the Cape Verde Islands west of Africa, and Jose, then 18 years old, had just signed on aboard the *Wanderer*, a 116-foot square-rigger out of New Bedford, Massachusetts, bound for the West Indies, the Canaries, and the southern seas to hunt the great whale.

"I had to take a chance," Jose told me. "Cape Verde was dry. We wait for the rain, but no rain comes, and people want to get out, like me." He recalled his inexperience: "Before I go on the *Wanderer*, I never see a whaling ship, never go inside a ship, never use an oar, nothing," he said. "The only thing was, when I left Cape Verde Islands, I know how to swim."

I met Jose and his wife, Maria—both Cape Verdeans—at their home in New Bedford, just inland from town, out of

sight of the sea. Southern New England probably has America's largest communities of Portuguese-Cape Verdeans. Their contact and seafaring have a long history here, dating back to the 16th century when men from the Azores sailed west to fish the Grand Banks. In the mid-19th century, many settled around New Bedford, Fall River, and Providence, Rhode Island, after working on the American whaling ships that stopped in the Azores and Cape Verde Islands for supplies and crew.

New Bedford flourished through the 1800s as the greatest whaling port in the world, its grand buildings lining the harbor and looking to sea like an anxious crowd awaiting the return of the ships. Seagoing New England first prospered on maritime commerce and the riches of the sea, on shipbuilding, and on the China trade—and on a whaling fleet that roamed the world. But by the time of Jose's voyage, the days of whaling had nearly ended. As a crewman on the *Wanderer*, the last American sailing ship to pursue the great leviathans, Jose is a living voice from a past era, one of a handful of men with firsthand memories of the old days of whaling.

"I'm the youngest one left. I'm 86 years," said Jose, who was also the youngest on the *Wanderer*. "At first they said I was too small, but then everybody wants me be-

cause I was not afraid; I climb the mast like a cat." He also rowed in the six-man longboats that chased the whales, sometimes for several days. "When you leave the mother ship to follow the whale, you don't know what's going to happen. Men were killed. You gotta be quiet and you gotta go quick so the mate can throw the lance. Then the whale goes down, down, and when he comes up—how many spouts? The whale pulls the boat fast, up and down we go. We all hold the line, but when the boat starts to pitch, you gotta loose up. Sometimes the rope gets so hot you gotta keep it wet with the water, or your hands will burn. When we kill the whale, we put a big flag on him for the ship to see," said Jose. "Then he's a whale. When he's alive, on the line, he's a monster."

After a year's voyage, the *Wanderer* returned to New Bedford, and Jose was told that if he wanted to immigrate to America, he had to make another whaling voyage, which he did, for five months, on the *Margarita*. For his 17 months' work at sea, Jose earned 30 dollars. "After that, when the captain told us we had to go back again on the sea to become citizens, we refused—we knew it was a trick," he told me. "He just wanted to make more money."

I made a brief visit with Jose and Maria to the Seamen's Bethel, the chapel in New Bedford immortalized by Herman Melville in *Moby Dick*, where whalemen went to pray before long voyages to distant seas unknown. Marble plaques around the chapel walls honor the memory of those lost far from home—off the coast of Africa, the Okhotsk Sea, the North Pacific, Calcutta, Cape Horn. A story on one plaque of a man dragged to the deep by a whale is said to have inspired Melville's great tale.

At the end of his brief whaling career,

Jose settled in New Bedford, where he worked for 24 years at the local cotton mill. He raised three children (none fishermen or sailors) who live nearby with their families, and although he has returned to Cape Verde to visit, his new roots are in New England. "I have many family here now," he says. "This is my home." He showed me a small harpoon on his wall. "My grandson made it for me," he said. "He likes to hear the stories of the whales."

U*nder a spreading chestnut-tree*
The village smithy stands . . .
Week in, week out,
from morn till night,
You can hear his bellows blow;
You can hear him swing his heavy sledge,
With measured beat and slow.
                    —*The Village Blacksmith*

The shuddering, pounding, mighty-machine power of America's industrial revolution seems to make the village smithy an image of a far gentler time. The revolution had its birthplace in New England, not far from Jose Ramos's home. Historians point to the Old Slater Mill, built in 1793, a pale yellow-and-white clapboard building on the Blackstone River in Pawtucket, Rhode Island, as the starting point of this "second revolution" that transformed American life.

The story begins with an Englishman named Samuel Slater, a shrewd business-man and manager. In 1789, at the age of 21, he completed an apprenticeship in Derbyshire, England, under a partner of Richard Arkwright, inventor of water-powered spinning machinery that was revolutionizing textile production in England. The specifications for Arkwright's equipment were considered so vital to England that trained mechanics or those with models or drawings of the machines were discouraged from emigrating.

Legend holds that, disguised as a farm laborer, with the shirt on his back and Arkwright's plans in his head, Slater sailed for the brand-new United States of America, having heard that there were many opportunities there for men with knowledge of the textile industry. Within months of Slater's arrival in 1789, Moses Brown, a wealthy Quaker from Providence, Rhode Island, had financed the young Englishman to duplicate and refine Arkwright's machinery, as well as his production systems, and in 1793 the present-day mill began operation in Pawtucket, a few miles north of Providence.

It was a turning point in America, then an agricultural nation with 95 percent of its population living in rural areas. Every home with a spinning wheel and a loom was its own textile factory. Within 30 years, Slater's technology, in myriad new forms, had spread along New England's rivers, up and down the East Coast and over the Appalachians, and with it, the new system of factory production that concentrated labor pools drew people in from the countryside and gave rise to new cities.

On a blustery fall day of gunflint skies, with the air full of spinning wheels of leaves flashing copper and gold, I visited the Slater Mill Historic Site, joining a tour led by historian and guide De Witt Kilgore. Inside an old home next to the mill, De Witt demonstrated the home-textile techniques the industrial revolution replaced—picking, carding, spinning, and weaving—but a few wooden pegs on the walls made another point. "They hung their clothes on these pegs," De Witt explained. "Before the industrial revolution, textiles were so expensive and most people had so few

articles of clothing that they had no need for closets."

In the dark and cavernous mill, De Witt moved around the room like the Wizard of Oz, setting in motion an amazing array of massive, clanking, humming machines: Lines of spools whirled in synchrony, growing fat with bright threads; looms banged and cloth appeared; and tricolored shoelaces formed before our eyes on a Maypole braider. We succumbed to the magical hypnosis of machines, and it left us all silent and mesmerized, with one amusing exception. Outside the mill I fell in step behind a couple from England who had taken the tour, and I heard the woman remark to her husband, "He filched the plans, as it were, you know. You can see these mills all over south Yorkshire."

Moses Brown's farsighted decision to back young Samuel Slater was one of many lucrative choices made by successive generations of a family whose long and diverse role in the shaping of New England is a microcosm of many strains of the region's history. From Chad Brown, the first ancestor who came in 1638, descendants have ranged from churchmen to congressmen, bankers to patriots, shipping magnates to architects, even Quaker abolitionists and slave traders—in the same generation. What stories are passed along in a family whose past is in our history books? What legends linger in the mind today, to consider for yourself, to tell your children?

At her home in Dedham, Massachusetts, I talked with Angela Brown Fischer, a direct descendant of Chad Brown, and the person to whom the management of family investments has been entrusted in this generation. She commutes from Dedham to her Providence office in a building designed by her ancestor, Joseph Brown, not far from the Nicholas Brown house, where she grew up, next to the historic John Brown mansion, adjacent to Brown University—named for her family in thanks for their first major gift to the school, seven generations ago.

"Our original ancestor, Chad Brown, was a minister who came to Boston for religious freedom," Angela said, "but he found the Puritan community in Boston so oppressive that he left Massachusetts in 1638 and joined the new settlement founded by Roger Williams, where Providence is today." Angela leaned back on the couch, reviewing family tales with a mix of humor and analysis. "You don't always listen with both ears when you're a kid," she continued, "and suddenly you find that your parents aren't around any more, and you have to interpret what you remember. I think family legends are like our national legends, in that we cherish certain stories, no matter how true they are."

The Brown family's era of greatest influence began a few generations after Chad, in the late 18th century. "The legendary brothers were four," Angela said. "John, Joseph, Nicholas, and Moses. Their father had died young, and they were raised by their Uncle Obadiah. They expanded on his speculation in shipping, really taking enormous risks. They sent out all these trading vessels, many of which failed to return. They had to face disease, storms, pirates—and they were just very lucky with their investments. After they made a certain amount of money, they diversified and got into candles, gunpowder for the Revolution—they kept up. It's like venture capital today."

Angela enumerated the generations, considering their investments in the light of history and the present, sprinkled with accounts of patriotism and moral dilemmas. "The brothers profited during the Revolution, with things that were needed for the war," she said. "But they didn't always agree. Moses became a Quaker and an abolitionist, whereas John had made some money off the slave trade, and he wasn't going to be deciding against slavery quite so soon. There were some heated arguments. Then Moses bankrolled this young Englishman, Slater, and weren't they lucky to have been there at the right moment, with money in their pockets?"

Although we were in Dedham, Angela often said "here" when she meant Providence, where her ties are strongest. "I think it's so important for Americans to understand their own past and where they came from," she said. "And I think it's so interesting that it took a TV show about a black family from Africa to bring home to all of us that roots do matter, that they give you something that we need more of in this country, and that is a sense of self."

Many people hold dear something from their family past—a reminder of an ancestor, a story, or a past time. Of the material objects in her home, Angela treasures most two sauceboats, dating from about 1760, that were part of John and Sarah Brown's wedding silver. She handed them to me to feel their weight. "They're not fancy," she said, "but aren't they heavy? They don't

shine like later silver that was buffed on machines. And oddly enough, John and Sarah picked a British silversmith, because it was more economical to buy in Europe then. If they had chosen Paul Revere, these would be ten times more valuable! But everything here was so expensive then, and American industry was all so new—in fact, it hadn't really been born."

O*ne, if by land, and two, if by sea;*
     And I on the opposite shore will be,
     Ready to ride and spread the alarm
Through every Middlesex village and farm.
                              —*Paul Revere's Ride*

I laughed at the directions I received in Concord, Massachusetts. "Meet me at the Old Buttrick place," Thomas Adams said on the phone. "Follow the road out from Concord green, past the Bullet Hole House, though naturally you won't see the hole. Go on by the rude bridge that arched the flood, and turn left up the hill to the Buttrick home. I'll be there. We'll travel the Battle Road to get an idea of just what happened on the 19th of April, 1775. It's terribly important," he added. "It's the most important four miles in American history."

Thomas Boylston Adams, descendant of our second and sixth presidents, John and John Quincy, and a relative of colonial firebrand Sam Adams, comes naturally by his interest in the American Revolution, and in particular in the preservation of the Battle Road between Lexington and Concord, the route Paul Revere rode with his warning of the British advance. It leads on to the Old North Bridge, where "the shot heard 'round the world" was fired—the legendary start of the Revolutionary War.

Along with the Old North Bridge, the land edging both sides of the Battle Road between Lexington and Concord—but not including the road itself—comprises the Minute Man National Historical Park. At park headquarters, ranger Dan Dattilio told me about the park. "It commemorates the place where a small group of men stood up against the most powerful country in the world because of what they believed in," he said. "And what they did here shaped the destiny of every American living today. Some parks protect a landscape for its own sake," he added, "but this park preserves an idea."

The National Park Service's long-range management plan for Minute Man Park calls for the Battle Road to be restored to its 18th-century appearance. "The idea is to take people back in time, for visitors to feel as if they are seated in an alcove of the past," Dan explained, "where they can sense the land as it was and imagine the events that took place here." The proposal has stirred local controversy. Since the park was established in 1959, the Battle Road has become a Boston commuter route, whizzing with cars; in addition to the eventual removal of several post-Revolutionary-era homes along the road, the management plan calls for cutting down trees, rebuilding stone walls, and for taking the road down to its original dirt bed.

Commuter traffic would be rerouted. It will take years to resolve the details and implement the plan, but as park superintendent Robert Nash told me, "The Battle Road is the heart of the park, and it's a major highway now. It's as if you had a park centered on a river valley, but the river itself was enclosed in a concrete tube."

A vocal proponent of the Park Service plan, Thomas Adams has a personal attachment to the Battle Road that goes beyond its historic value. The road has woven a path through his 79 years, looping from his boyhood to the present. "I used to ride a pony to school down this road," he told me as we set off from the Buttrick House. "I lived in Lincoln, just south of here, and my parents felt that I should go to school in Concord, which is the center of all learning, as you've probably discovered. I started riding to school, five miles each way, when I was six years old, in 1916. This road was tarred then, but the edges were soft, and you could canter your horse right along the side."

We passed the Emerson house, next to the Old North Bridge, as well as Nathaniel Hawthorne's Old Manse, the Alcott family's Orchard House, where Louisa May Alcott wrote *Little Women,* and The Wayside, where all of them but Ralph Waldo Emerson once lived, and where Margaret Sidney wrote the Five Little Peppers books.

Every bend in the road seemed to have a significant site, and as we crept along, with cars wailing past us, Thomas Adams sketched a picture of the British march to the Old North Bridge and then the retreat back down the Battle Road, all the way to Boston's Bunker Hill, the signal fight of all-out war.

We stopped at the Meriam House, the scene of the first fighting after the exchange of shots at the bridge. "This is the beginning of the trouble right here," Thomas explained. "The bridge could have been just another skirmish, but unwisely the last of the British soldiers passing here wheeled and fired at the Minute Men, who were hidden behind the sheds and rocks. Then it was for real, and this is what made the war. Of course they didn't know then what was starting," he said. "The people who fought were concerned with one thing: Who are these strangers, and what are they doing coming out here with their guns?

"Long after the Revolution, one of the last colonial veterans told a historian why they fought, saying, 'What we meant in going for those Redcoats was this: We had always governed ourselves, and we always meant to. They didn't mean we should.'"

Much of the landscape around the Meriam House is forested. "At the time of the war, there were almost no trees here," Thomas said. "This was all under cultivation. Everything had to be grown right here in New England, and every inch of arable land was farmed. Even when I was a boy, this countryside was all cultivated. The land was open, and you could see a great distance, as you could in 1775. With stone walls everywhere dividing the fields the British army had to follow the road. They had no choice. It's hard to imagine now, with all these trees, but everyone who moved across this land was exposed."

To see the site where Paul Revere was captured, we dashed across the road in a break between long rivers of cars. "It's worth your life to see this spot," Thomas said. "When I was a small boy of nine my Uncle Harry showed me this place. With the moon in its third quarter, here ended the midnight ride of Paul Revere.

"There were two other riders—Dawes and Prescott. Dawes turned back when Revere was halted by a British patrol, but Prescott cleared the stone wall and rode on to alarm Concord. The word spread, and thousands of Minute Men came from all over the countryside, throughout the next day, to this road. Eventually the British let Paul Revere go, because it was just such a nuisance to have him around, but they took his horse. No one knows what became of Paul Revere's horse."

We reached a place where a length of the original roadbed still exists and walked along it. "Now if you can just imagine all of this cleared of trees, with nothing but the stone walls," Thomas said, "perhaps you can picture how completely invincible the British army would have seemed, marching out from Boston. You would have seen them coming, far in the distance. Psychologically they were perfectly overwhelming. They presented a fine sight coming with their fifes and drums, and they made fine music. Imagine seeing them marching, resplendent in their red uniforms, with the immense power of the British Empire behind them. Imagine defying them and all they stood for. Apparently, it was a perfectly crazy thing to do."

We headed back down the Battle Road, retracing our route to the Buttrick House. "Amazingly, the lay of the road is the same," Thomas said. "It hasn't changed since I rode my pony here. But as the landscape appears now, visitors get a totally wrong impression of what happened here. They would think, 'What's so very heroic about the colonials standing behind all these trees and potting those poor cows as they went by?' That's why it's so important to restore the landscape to its former appearance. Every American should be able to envision it as it was."

For a personal glimpse of how it was for him, Thomas took me to the Adams family home in Quincy, now a historic site administered by the National Park Service. Generations of Adams family possessions and memorabilia fill the house, and as we roamed the rooms, beyond the velvet ropes, Thomas offered tidbits of history blended with memories.

We passed a row of portraits. "This is Abigail Brooks Adams in London before the Civil War," he said. "As you see, she's beginning to look like Queen Victoria.

And here's her husband. The signature of the family is a bald head," he said, rubbing his own.

We entered the upstairs study. "Uncle Henry, who wrote *The Education of Henry Adams*, says that he remembers his grandfather, John Quincy Adams, with a perpetual ink stain on his right hand. So you can imagine him sitting here at his desk, with his back to the fire, dipping his pen into the inkwell, the everlasting ink stain on his finger, writing, writing, writing. And these are his glasses." He picked up a pair of small, squarish spectacles and handed them to me. "Look through them," he said. The room blurred, but fine print on the desk grew large. "They were magnifying glasses for reading," Thomas explained. "They came from Holland, which was the center for optics then. John Adams probably brought them.

"The legends say that John Adams died there," he said, pointing to a wing chair near the desk. "He was resting there on July 4th, 1826. John Quincy had recently been elected president, and on that morning, the 50th anniversary of the Declaration of Independence, John Adams collapsed in that chair. They carried him to bed, where he died, murmuring, 'Thomas Jefferson still lives.' Strangely, Jefferson, down in Virginia, had died that same morning, just before John Adams collapsed."

In the tall stone library adjacent to the house, we perused the vast collection of Adams books. "These are our real family jewels," Thomas said. "I spent a great many hours of my youth here." We selected books and read the notes John Quincy Adams had made in the margins. On a page in Bolingbrokes's *Remarks on the History of England*, he had written, "The great who pretend to aim at glory alone have always been detected sooner or later in schemes for power and wealth. . . . What a mighty maze is man."

"Can you climb?" Thomas called to me, as he scrambled up a ladder to a second-story catwalk around the library. "This is my favorite place. This is where the novels are, the poems and stories of fairies and enchantments. See how tiny these books are? You could carry them in your pocket. John Adams once wrote in one of these books to John Quincy, 'With a poet in your pocket, you will never be alone.' I think that's very nice, don't you?"

Outside the library door a tour group waited. "I think it's terribly important to know as much as we can about our history," Thomas Adams said. "With all the lovely notes in the margins, just as they were written. I think that trying to understand the times as they really were helps us on our way." If the places and voices and remembrances of New England's past each stood like Sister Frances's candle in the night, perhaps our way would shine.

Mists of Plymouth Harbor enwrap the Mayflower II, *a reproduction of the vessel that carried 102*

Pilgrims from England to the New World's rocky shores.

It's all in the Mayflower *family when descendants of Pilgrim
William Bradford gather in Plymouth for a reunion. Family
historian May Ellen Pogue (above) examines genealogical charts
with Laurence Boothby, also a Bradford descendant. At Burial
Hill cemetery, the family assembles around a memorial to
Bradford, governor of Plymouth for more than 30 years and
author of the colony's first history. Though the General Society
of* Mayflower Descendants *has some 25,000 registered
members, genealogical researchers estimate that 20 to 30 million
Americans may have a* Mayflower *ancestor.*

First New Englanders proclaim their heritage at the annual powwow in Portland, Connecticut, where Wampanoag tribal dancer Nanepashemet (left) cradles his infant son. A member of the tribe that greeted the Mayflower Pilgrims when they landed, Nanepashemet works as a research

associate at Plimoth Plantation. In Mashpee, on Cape Cod, Wampanoag matriarch Amelia Bingham wears a shawl she embroidered with designs representing the meaning of her tribe's name, "People of the First Light," a geographic metaphor used by several East Coast tribes.

Memories of witch-hunting haunt the town of Salem as well as
the writings of New England author Nathaniel Hawthorne, a
Salem native buried in Concord (below). Descendant of a witch-
trial judge, Hawthorne grew up with the legend that the judge
had been cursed by a witch, a tale he told in his novel The House
of the Seven Gables, *named for his cousin's home (above). In
nearby Danvers, a tree casts its gnarled shadow on the home of
Rebecca Nurse, who was hanged as a witch in 1692 (right).*

Bright lights and skyscrapers encircle the Old State House in the heart of downtown Boston (right). The building, near the site of the 1770 Boston Massacre, served as a venue for pre-Revolutionary War public meetings and debates. The roll call of famous native Bostonians includes Benjamin Franklin (above), who, along with such luminaries as John Hancock, Samuel Adams, and Ralph Waldo Emerson, attended the Boston Public Latin School (below), founded in 1635 as America's first public school.

Walls of books read by generations of his ancestors surround Thomas Boylston Adams in the stone library of the Adams House in Quincy, Massachusetts. A descendant of the country's second and sixth presidents—John and John Quincy—Thomas Adams recalls childhood days browsing among the library's rows of leather-bound volumes, "the real family jewels." Both the painting and the bust (below) portray John Quincy Adams, whose books fill the library. Walking sticks once belonged to members of the Adams family.

Tranquil autumn softens a former scene of war. Here, between Lexington and Concord in Massachusetts, colonial Minute Men confronted British troops at the Old North Bridge (above right) on April 19, 1775—the legendary start of the American Revolution. Redcoats and colonial militia fired from opposite ends of the bridge, a beginning immortalized by Emerson as "the shot heard 'round the world." A statue in Lexington (above left) honors the Minute Men—a volunteer militia prepared to fight at a minute's notice. Members of the Lexington Minute Men (right), a reenactment group, raise a toast in a nearby tavern.

Keepers of the Shaker faith continue the ascetic sect's spirit and way of life. In
Sabbathday Lake, Maine, home to eight Shakers, Sister Frances Carr (above) holds
a portrait of Eldress Prudence Stickney, who offered her early spiritual guidance. A
museum (below) reflects the spare simplicity of Shaker designs. In Canterbury
Shaker Village in New Hampshire, tour guide Ed Beargeon visits with Eldress
Bertha Lindsay (right), one of the village's two surviving Shakers.

Weather, water, and time take their toll on ships abandoned on the Maine coast near Wiscasset. The last

four-masted schooners built in the U.S., Hesper *and* Luther Little *have moldered here since the 1930s.*

In Memory of
CAPT. WM. SWAIN,
Associate
Master of the Christopher
Mitchell of Nantucket.
This worthy man,
after fastning to a whale,
was carried overboard by
the line, and drowned
May 19ᵗ 1844.
in the 49ᵗ Year of his age.

Be ye also ready; for in such an hour as ye
think not, the Son of man cometh.

From a ship's-prow pulpit, the Reverend C. L. Newbert speaks in the Seamen's Bethel in New Bedford. In the 19th-century heyday of whaling and sailing, when New England vessels roamed the world's seas, whalers gathered here to pray before a voyage. The pulpit matches one described in Herman Melville's Moby Dick, *an epic of whaling that may have been inspired in part by a plaque on the chapel wall (below left). At Mystic Seaport in Connecticut (below), elegant restorations of sailing vessels evidence the skill that brought fame to New England shipbuilders.*

Family portraits frame Angela Brown Fischer at the Nicholas Brown House, a historic mansion in Providence, Rhode Island—and the home where Angela grew up. The Brown family's prominence dates from the success of four brothers who profited from the sale

of munitions during the American Revolution and also from the 18th-century China trade. A room in the nearby John Brown House (left) displays a collection of Oriental furnishings and objects representative of the era when China-trade treasures furnished the homes of New England's wealthy. The Browns—for whom Brown University is named—later invested in the technology introduced by Englishman Samuel Slater that helped give rise to New England's 19th-century industrial revolution.

By the falls of the Blackstone River in Rhode Island, lights glitter in the windows of the Old Slater Mill,

at right, birthplace of the factory system for manufacturing cotton cloth in America.

II

ON A ROCKY AND FOGBOUND COAST

Text and Photographs by Tor Eigeland

It was like driving into a giant cotton ball. I braked and turned on the headlights. And as if the fog were not surprise enough, the temperature suddenly fell. It seemed to go down about 20 degrees within just a few feet. Typical of the New England coast, I thought. I was driving into Lubec, Maine—the easternmost town in the United States—and, as often happens here, warm inland air had clashed with cool ocean breezes from the icy Bay of Fundy, creating a cold dense fog.

A thousand years ago my Viking ancestors braved the North Atlantic in wooden boats. They must have penetrated fogbanks as thick as this one and explored coastlines as mysterious. Did they feel daunted by this new coast, not knowing what adventures they would encounter?

I know I did, for ahead of me lay 6,130 miles of New England shoreline—a coast that bends and twists along the mainland and among numberless islands from northern Maine to southwestern Connecticut. Maine, with 3,478 miles, accounts for more than half the total.

Form served function in sleek historic watercraft: This sharpie (right, foreground), afloat at the Mystic Seaport Museum in Connecticut, once sped competing oystermen to market. Above, a schooner sails in a regatta.

I had heard that many of the people of Maine would be reluctant to talk with a "foreigner." It didn't take me long to realize how inaccurate that was; I was reminded of people I meet who think reindeer and polar bears wander city streets in my native Norway. During a lifetime of traveling throughout the world I have never encountered friendlier, more helpful people than in New England. Reluctant to talk? On the contrary. I would still be in Maine today, talking about herring, blueberries, and life in general, had not my editors kept saying: "You're still in *Maine?*"

Though New England is not a big area, Maine is so far from Connecticut that people here, asked if they are New Englanders, will hesitate and say, "Well, sort of."

Which is what Carl Stover said when I accompanied him on a sardine boat, the nearly 70-year-old *Medric,* out to a dozen weirs, or traps, to harvest fish for the R. J. Peacock Canning Company. So why was Carl only "sort of" a New Englander? "People around here just don't think of themselves that way," he said. "Besides, I'm actually a sort of double-ender. That's what we call people who were born in Canada but live over here, or vice versa. The name comes from these boats, because they're pointed on both ends."

At the weirs a large hose unceremoniously vacuumed struggling masses of silver fish out of the nets and into the hull of the boat. "But these aren't sardines," I protested. "They're herring."

"They're herring until they go into the cans," Carl said. "Then they're sardines. They change real quick." Indeed, I later learned, a sardine can be any one of several small or immature herring.

I saw what may have been the same herring later as they floated along a conveyor in the Peacock Company's ancient red barnlike building. Women with incredibly nimble fingers cut and packed the sardines at such a furious pace it was almost impossible to see what they were doing. Some rocked rhythmically back and forth on their feet as their fingers flew.

Not far from Lubec, at a remote corner of Cobscook Bay, I had a momentary scare. A new acquaintance named Mike was going clamming, and I went with him. The tide, which in the nearby Bay of Fundy can rise and fall by more than 30 feet, was out. We walked outward from shore, splashing through mud for half an hour, sinking in with every step. Mike showed me the holes in the surface that indicated the presence of buried clams and started digging with his hands. After a while the fog came drifting in. Mike stayed. I had to return to Lubec. I splashed and skidded toward shore as fast as I could. I lost sight of Mike. The fog thickened. I could see little beyond my own muddy feet. I was losing my sense of direction. I kept imagining a rushing tide. . . . Then the fog lifted for a few moments, and I could see the tree-lined shore, and safety.

Cutler, a nicely sheltered fishing town a few miles down the coast from Lubec, has a white town hall high on a hill that boasts a library and a fine view of the harbor. But an oddity occupies its basement: a lobster hatchery. Amid containers of different sizes and different colors, some bubbling like simmering soup, I found Andy Patterson.

"Basically, we're giving mother nature a hand here," he said. "The number of lobsters caught off Maine has recently stayed more or less the same, even though there are many more traps being set. We're concerned that the stock of lobsters is being

stretched to its limit, so we hope to raise and put overboard about 200,000 baby lobsters this year, up and down the coastline."

According to Brian Beal, a young marine biologist from the University of Maine at Machias, the survival rate of lobsters at the hatchery is between 40 and 50 percent, whereas in the sea probably just 1 percent of young lobsters survive to adulthood.

Brian knew everything and everyone along that stretch of coast, for his family has lived in the Beals Island–Jonesport area for five or six generations. One afternoon we visited Uncle Miltie's Fish Market just outside Jonesport, and Uncle Miltie turned out to be Brian's father. He gave me a sample of what he called "Down East chewing gum," dried and lightly salted strips of codfish—very chewy, initially shocking, then delicious and habit-forming.

A teacher and a researcher, Brian runs the lobster hatchery at Cutler as well as a clam-breeding project on Beals Island, both for the university. "In Washington County we now have private aquaculture, mostly in mussels and salmon, which are new businesses here. And we also have public aquaculture—the clam- and lobster-hatchery projects.

"Norwegians were very involved in starting up the salmon farms. They had the experience and the capital, and we had the pure water, the great flushing action from our tremendous tides, and the favorable economic conditions."

But, Brian told me, soft-shell clams are still the major marine resource in Washington County. Unfortunately, as with nearly every other oceanic resource, clam beds are being threatened by pollution and overfishing. So the hatchery-reared clam project on Beals Island is a ten-town community effort aimed at resupplying exhausted clam beds.

An ingenious method induces the clams to spawn. Males and females are kept together in a tank of water at about 55°F. "Then," explained Brian, "we drain that water out and allow water about 20 degrees warmer to flow over the clams. It is such a thermal shock that within two hours the clams have spawned." The previous year, 1987, had been extremely successful. "We spawned eight million clams instead of the six million we had planned on," said Brian.

Beals Island seems a proper setting for the hatchery. Everything relates to the sea and to fishing. Boats line every shore and are parked alongside cars and trucks in driveways. Houses are modest but well kept, and multicolored buoys and lobster traps brighten gardens and flower beds. In some yards, broad-beamed lobster boats are taking shape.

One morning I set out with Harry Beal, one of the best lobstermen around. It was a clear day, and harbor seals were sunning on the rocks. The sea shone like molten lead, and in it bobbed Harry's yellow-black-and-red lobster buoys. As nimble and quick with his hands as a sardine packer, Harry winched in traps, grabbed the lobsters, and popped rubber bands around their claws so they couldn't damage one another. He caught a number of crabs, too, which were thrown into a separate bucket. He pitched snails, sea urchins, starfish, and rocks back into the sea while complaining loudly about horseflies "as big as sea gulls." Baited with fresh herring, the traps splashed back overboard.

From the east side of Frenchman Bay, 60

or 70 miles down the coast, you can easily see the Atlantic seaboard's tallest coastal mountain rising on Mount Desert Island. Two different worlds lie within easy sight of each other here. The west side of Mount Desert Island is still Down East and relatively unspoiled. The east side is spectacularly beautiful but busy and commercial.

In the evening I drove through Acadia National Park and up the winding road to the peak of 1,530-foot Cadillac Mountain. The parking lot on top was jammed, but people spread out so there was room enough for all to enjoy the evening sun and a panorama of sky, sea, land, and islands. Frenchman Bay, Schoodic Point, the Cranberry Isles, the Camden and Rockland areas—all were clearly visible below.

While sunset approached, a warmly wrapped crowd gathered and sat on the rocks, as if awaiting a performance. As the last sliver of orange-red sun dipped below the horizon, there was enthusiastic applause from the mountaintop.

At Mount Desert Island's Southwest Harbor beauty of a quite different sort is produced. Built to transform wind power into speed, some of the world's finest sailboats have been crafted here since 1932 by the Hinckley Company. The firm's present line—the Bermuda 40, the Sou'wester 42, 51, and 59, the Competition 42—are all made with fiberglass hulls and decks.

Careful attention to a thousand details is a trademark here. Woodwork of teak, mahogany, cherry, ash—the choice is the buyer's—are sanded 6 or 8, even as many as 16 times. Hardware shines like a jeweler's display, as do a stem fitting of cast stainless steel and portlights of tempered glass.

Totally different was the barn-red and barnlike wooden-boat building—the Rockport Apprenticeshop—that I visited a few days later. Apprentices and master builders here were going about the business of crafting traditional wooden boats: a 26-foot Shetland Islands boat; a Washington County peapod, which is a kind of open Maine fishing boat; a Friendship sloop. Someone was even working on a Norwegian pram—a small rowboat that was the yacht of my dreams when I was a boy at home in Norway.

Steve McAllister, associate director of the Apprenticeshop, told me: "A few years ago Lance Lee, founder and director, saw that all the old-time boatbuilders were dying, taking their skills with them, and that young people weren't being trained to replace them. Boat shops were only marginally profitable, and owners couldn't afford to take on untrained people, even at minimum wages. So Lance started the apprentice shop to teach young people. Now we get students from all over the world."

A boat is the only way to get to tiny Monhegan Island, about ten miles south of Port Clyde. By chance I met George Cabot there. His grandfather built the house that he and his wife, Karen, live in. Over coffee and sandwiches on the porch, George told me about the island, which is barely a square mile in area. "There are no private cars and few trucks here, except for those of the fishermen. The island is peaceful, has great natural beauty, and the local people are totally honest," he said. Only lobstermen and their families, a few innkeepers, an artist, and a big herd of deer live here all year. At least 150 species of birds have been seen on the island.

One morning before the sun was quite up I walked along a muddy trail to the cliffs on the east side of the island. There were

deer tracks and wildflowers in the meadows, and pines towered above. Abruptly the forest ended and the open Atlantic spread out below me. As the orange-red sun rose out of the dead-calm sea, there was perfect silence. For a moment it felt like the beginning of time.

Before year-round settlement began on Monhegan in 1623, the Algonquin Indians came here in the summers to fish. "They caught lobster and other shellfish and fished for swordfish," Cynthia Hagar Krusell of the Monhegan Museum told me. "We can tell that from the artifacts we've found—spears they used for going after swordfish, for instance."

Artifacts of another sort—signs for pizza, Chinese food, Syrian subs and calzones—greeted me as I drove into Portland on the shores of Casco Bay. Portland's old waterfront has undergone a major face-lift after a long period of decay, when land and air transport gradually displaced ships. Now small shops, boutiques, condominiums, and seafood restaurants are rejuvenating the waterfront.

I parked at the docks and stepped aboard *Longfellow II*, a tour boat captained by Rodney E. Ross III, "founder and majority stockholder of the Longfellow Cruise Line." Casco Bay, 18 miles wide at its mouth, is dotted with the "Calendar Islands." The Federal Writers' Project guide to Maine says: "Any bay native will say that the islands number 365, 'one for every day in the year.' By official count there are only 222 'big enough for a man to get out and stand on.'" Their names are fascinating: Junk of Pork, Pound of Tea, Stepping Stones, Brown Cow, Pumpkin Knob.

On its route, *Longfellow II* passed just below the Portland Head Light, Maine's oldest lighthouse, which was completed in 1791—the first lighthouse commissioned by the new federal government of George Washington. As well as being a lifesaver, this tall, sturdy guardian has witnessed many a maritime disaster. During one ferocious storm in 1869, about 20 vessels wrecked when the light's foghorn was destroyed by crashing waves.

Captain Ross pointed out what to me was Casco Bay's most intriguing sight: a strange, slender, pyramidal structure built of rocks on Little Mark Island in the outer part of the bay. It was erected as a navigational device by the federal government in 1827 and has since been painted white by the Coast Guard. "But there are still people who believe it was built by the Vikings," Captain Ross told me. Another reminder of my Viking ancestors!

The coast of Maine ended for me just south of Old Orchard Beach—seven miles of sandy, sunny, deserted shoreline, like an empty Coney Island—in Kennebunkport, newly in the news as President Bush's summer home. The town itself, a busy fishing port, is also full of boutiques and shops, and the coast is lined with the elegant mansions of the wealthy, as well as hotels and inns.

I crossed into New Hampshire at Portsmouth, the state's only seaport. In the quiet heart of its historic downtown, I found the inn that I remember as the best of all I stayed in in New England. Originally built as a home by businessman John Sise in

1881, it has been converted into the 32-room Sise Inn and decorated with Queen Anne and Victorian furniture. The antiques are real; the plants are real; gently moving ceiling fans quietly stir the air; and skylights fill the rooms with light. There are large, comfortable beds and discreetly hidden cable-television sets. Everything works, including the friendly and professional staff.

A little reluctant to leave, I entered Massachusetts at Cape Ann, technically an island, and visited its main city, Gloucester, the oldest seaport in the United States. Home to some 28,000, Gloucester feels old, looks old, and smells of the sea and fish and, oddly, I thought, of thyme. It is a real port, though, with a far-ranging deep-water fishing fleet. Italian and Portuguese names are common.

Gloucester is full of surprises. You pass a waterfront industrial plant of some kind but find a chic restaurant next door. You think you're in the city but, making a turn, find yourself on a winding country lane. Then there's a beach, then a residential area of old seamen's homes. Eastern Point is dotted with palatial mansions and enormous gardens.

This coast once was rich in oil—the oil of whales. And ironically these gentle giants are again contributing to the economy of the northern Massachusetts coast. On a brilliant, calm day I went whale watching aboard the sturdy *Privateer,* run by Seven Seas, of Gloucester. As we approached the Stellwagen Bank—where whales often feed on six-inch silvery fish called sand lance—a couple of whales spouted two or three miles away. Then a humpback breached completely out of the water.

As we got closer, whales surfaced and spouted all around us. People laughed and shouted with delight. "Did you *see* that?" Then a sound: *pfffff,* from a whale blowing heavily on one side of the ship; and *pfffff,* from another on the other side. The sound of the huge mammals blowing and breathing nearby was awesome.

Often a humpback would skim slowly along the surface with its mouth wide open, the inside clearly visible, feeding. Sea gulls flapped alongside, trying to catch fish brought up by the whales. A few gulls caught rides, perching momentarily on the big animals' heads.

When the whales dove, their flukes stuck up out of the water before vanishing with a splash. Since every fluke is different—most have nicks and scars—the whales are identified by them. These had names: Sirius, Tassel, Salt, Pegasus.

The playful, 40-foot humpbacks were the stars of the show, but we also saw the much larger finbacks, some smaller minke whales, and a few leaping dolphins.

Privateer's young captain, Sebastian Lovasco, Jr., comes from a family of fishermen and, on our way back to port, he told me about some of the problems of Gloucester's fleet. "Simply, there are too many fishermen and too few fish," he said. "The fishermen are getting very discouraged. Their equipment gets more and more sophisticated and expensive, yet they catch fewer fish. They have to travel long distances to crowded and overfished banks."

Some fishermen, desperate and in debt, have scuttled their boats to collect insurance. Others have fallen even farther and stand convicted of smuggling drugs.

Farther down the coast, at Marblehead, I had an encounter with the forces of law and order but of a positive nature. I stopped to ask directions of a policeman, and a few minutes later he caught up with me and pulled me over. Knowing that I was taking photographs, Sergeant Brian Hitchcock offered to help. "It occurs to me," he said, "that the best shot of the Marblehead Harbor is from the top of Abbot Hall, our town hall. If you like, I'll get you up there."

Not only did he do that, but he also took me for a tour of the town in his cruiser. Once a bustling, working port, Marblehead now is a pleasure-boat center, and shipyards have largely vanished. But there are a number of sailmakers in Marblehead, and Brian dropped me off at one of them, North Sails, where I met David Curtis, himself a renowned sailor.

"A lot of the competitors in the Olympics last year used our sails," he told me. "They're all hand cut, hand stitched, and hand glued. It's a highly labor-intensive business." North Sails at Marblehead makes roughly 1,500 sails a year. Regular sails are dacron, but big spinnakers are made today of a new lightweight nylon. Sails were shuttled back and forth between different parts of the shop before being put in bags and dispatched out the door.

Another act of kindness helped me get a good view of Boston Harbor. When captain Peter Nugent of the tour boat *Gracious Lady* found out I was working, he gave me a trip around the harbor, even though I was his only customer. We joined a fray of commuter ferries, sailboats, oil tankers, tugboats, and freighters cruising the busy waters, past the new Fish Pier, past the World Trade Center, past condominiums. Helicopters overhead whirred back and forth across the Charles River to Logan International Airport, where a steady stream of jetliners took off and landed. From a distance Boston's new waterfront skyline gleamed impressively in the sun.

It was still dark the next morning when I sped out of the same harbor aboard a Coast Guard utility boat on its way to Boston Light, America's first lighthouse, built in 1716. And, as young lighthouse-keeper Dennis Dever of the Coast Guard told me, "It will also be the *last* manned lighthouse in the U.S. It's scheduled to be fully automated by early 1990. I should still be on duty here then, so I'm likely to be the last lighthouse keeper in the country."

Together we climbed the 76 steps to a balcony below the lantern. The Boston skyline loomed nine miles away. "The lighthouse was blown up by the British in 1776 when they pulled out of Boston during the Revolution," Dennis said. "It was rebuilt in 1783 and raised 14 feet in 1859.

"The area is full of wrecks," he added. "The seas here can be fierce. During a storm in 1978 the lighthouse keepers had to abandon their living quarters—they were waist deep in water—and retreat to the base of the lighthouse itself, which is built higher up."

Practically within sight of the lighthouse is another, very different world. An island since the construction of the Cape Cod Canal in 1916, the sickle-shaped, sandy Cape Cod peninsula juts far out into the Atlantic. Blessed with safe harbors, 585 miles of shoreline, and great natural beauty, the cape traditionally provided refuge for mariners and a safe base for fishermen.

Now, easy access across three bridges has made it a vacation playground that taxes to the limit everything from hotels and motels to shops, roads, and beaches. Increased tourism and more residents have brought with them new shopping centers and condominiums that are encroaching on the little island's fragile natural beauty.

The attack on the cape has been two-pronged: from the sea as well as from people. David William Stout of the Coast Guard Station at Provincetown told me: "Out at Highland Light, where we're on top of a 120-foot escarpment, we lost about ten feet of ground to erosion in just one storm a few years ago. In some places there's as much as six feet of loss a year."

Provincetown itself is well protected inside the top of the cape, where Long Point wraps halfway around it. Slightly seedy and a little honky-tonk, Provincetown may be the most colorful town I visited on the New England coast. Kitschy shops and restaurants line the sidewalks, along with bars, cabarets, hotels, and inns. Provincetown's permanent population hovers around 5,000, but that figure multiplies tenfold in summer.

A curious community, it is a mixture of fishermen of Portuguese descent and their families, and writers and artists. John Dos Passos, Tennessee Williams, and Sinclair Lewis all wrote here.

In sharp contrast to Provincetown is the dramatic natural beauty of the Cape Cod National Seashore, a park covering roughly the entire length of the eastern shore. Martha Lyon, a ranger with the National Park Service, took me on a tour of some of the cape. For the better part of a day we bounced along beaches caressed by a gentle Atlantic and ground through desertlike dunes in the interior. We visited freshwater ponds among the dunes, havens for birds and birdwatchers. Martha and I had skipped lunch, so we dined on wild cranberries, beach plums, and the biggest, reddest rose hips I ever saw.

Cape Cod is home to others concerned with conservation: The National Marine Fisheries Service's Northeast Fisheries Center is at Woods Hole. Having heard tales of woe from fishermen along the whole coast, I stopped in. "I would say that the status of the resources on which the fishermen—particularly the offshore fishermen—depend is as bad as it has ever been," said Dr. Fredric M. Serchuk, chief of New England Offshore Fishery Resources Investigation. "Times are tough now, and they're going to get tougher. The traditional resources are overfished."

A recent study of the codfish, one of the most important as well as one of the most resilient sea-bottom fish caught by New England fishermen, was alarming. "On Georges Bank we found that only about 30 percent of the adult codfish alive at the beginning of 1987 survived the fishing season. Normally that's not enough to sustain a viable population. This is bad news, for the codfish really is a bulwark of the fishing industry here."

Pollution is another insult to the coastal waters of New England, according to John B. Pearce, deputy director of the center. Toxic PCBs and petroleum hydrocarbons have been found in the tissues of some marine animals, he told me. Other pollutants, ranging from toxic metals to excessive nutrients, make up what has been called a witch's brew of hazardous substances that can be found in industrialized areas along the coast. It's a serious situation, he told me, but not yet dangerous to humans.

The crush of people toward the coast and the development they bring with them cause other problems. A short ferry hop south of Woods Hole I found a dynamic man with strong views on the costs of development. Gus Ben David, a native of Martha's Vineyard and the director of the

Massachusetts Audubon Society's Felix Neck Wildlife Sanctuary at Edgartown, spoke for many along the coast. "Cape Cod and Martha's Vineyard are victims of their own beauty," he told me. "The sheer numbers of new arrivals are changing the whole makeup of the community and the way we have lived here." He voiced a lament I had heard along the entire coast: "As property values rise, so do taxes, so unless people are really wealthy, they can barely afford to own land. Farmers are being taxed off their farms, off the land they love."

Gay Head, the westernmost point of Martha's Vineyard, is famous for the colors and moods of its cliffs, for its sunsets, and for the Wampanoag Indians. They achieved official status as a tribe only recently, when a settlement was reached with the federal government. "As far as the government was concerned, we didn't exist," Gladys Widdiss of the Wampanoag Tribal Council, told me. "Well, *we* knew we existed. There are about 580 Wampanoag, about half on Martha's Vineyard and the others scattered on the mainland. So in 1972 we filed suit to recover tribal common lands, and in 1987 we were awarded full recognition as a tribe and about 450 acres of tribal lands." Some of the most valuable real estate in the world, it might be added.

"So we're starting to make some progress," said Donald Widdiss, president of the tribal council. "But when *we* talk about progress, we're talking about *stopping* some things. Like overdevelopment and the misuse of the land, or like the slow destruction of the town of Gay Head. It was

getting so folks couldn't afford to live there." Chief Donald Malonson, Gladys and Don Widdiss, and Luther Madison, medicine man, took me to see their wild cranberry bogs and the places where they scallop, clam, and fish. At Herring Creek, Chief Malonson joked about catches of the past: "I've seen so many herring come up this creek they'd push each other up onto the banks."

Gladys added: "We used to lie on the bank with nets and scoop 'em up. Some of the older people used to dry them. All they did was take the herring and put a stick through its gills. At every house there'd be strings of herring hanging out to dry."

I left Martha's Vineyard regretfully, for the little island had shown me delightful secret corners and an enormous variety of scenery, wildlife, moods, people, towns, and social situations.

Rhode Island presented a similarly intriguing variety. Only 48 miles long and 37 miles wide, the Ocean State is dominated by 384 miles of shoreline. Its worlds are diverse: Sakonnet Point, where the only living beings I saw were two men and a woman fishing from the breakwater; Newport's grand mansions; Electric Boat, the nuclear-submarine division of General Dynamics at Quonset Point.

At Newport I checked into the Hotel Viking and drove off once again on the trail of my elusive ancestors. The Stone Tower, a curious round structure with eight arches on ground level and a superstructure built atop it, is in Touro Park. A sign says it was probably a mill built around 1660 by the

first governor of Rhode Island, Benedict Arnold. But the sign continues: "Legend ascribes its erection to the Vikings during their supposed visit about A.D. 1000."

About four million visitors a year cross the Newport Bridge onto the island, and on any given summer day there are thousands of pleasure boats in the harbor. "It's hard to describe how crowded it gets," said Harbor Master Mark Hastings. "Even on a weekday. Everybody's goin' all over the place. There are so many knuckleheads out there you have to see it to believe it. I have to take a weekend off in August. I go to Maine and hide in the woods."

Newport Harbor, once a major trading port, is being transformed with amazing speed from a working port to one for leisure boats, "dockominiums," condominiums, time-share residences, big hotels, restaurants, and boutiques. Fishermen will have new and expanded facilities away from the old docks, but some businesses are hanging on at the old Newport wharves. One is Christie's, a classic seafood restaurant that gets all my stars for excellence and atmosphere.

Another is Ronnie Fatulli's Aquidneck Lobster Company, which handles about two million pounds of live lobsters a year. "As a kid, before we bought this, I used to sell ice cream here," Ronnie told me. "This used to be a coal wharf, a real old wharf. The Fatulli company will be here as long as I'm alive." He had his own ideas about what was happening to Newport. "They're trying to make a little Manhattan out of it. There's so much money to be made, they don't think about the good of the city."

The majority of Rhode Islanders depend, in one way or another, on the sea for their livings. Tourism is big business, but Narragansett Bay hums with other activity as well. Lobstering, fishing, shipbuilding, and the harvesting of quahog clams are traditional industries here, and the quahog is the most important product from the bay. In 1986 quahogs provided about three million pounds of clam meat. Clammers harvest them by hand from open boats, using rakes that may be 70 feet long.

Huge barges dock at Electric Boat on Quonset Point, then depart with monstrous hull cylinders, sections of the nuclear submarines that are assembled at Groton, Connecticut. Tankers, freighters, and container ships destined for Providence and Quonset Point ply the bay.

Wines are made on Prudence Island in the middle of the bay, and also at peaceful Sakonnet. Some are good, and often their names are even better: Windswept Red, America's Cup, Eye of the Storm, Spinnaker White, Compass Rose.

Rhode Island also has a "backside," as it is called, best seen from the air. Along the entire southern shore from Point Judith to Watch Hill stretches a string of shallow salt ponds, separated from the sea by fragile sand-barrier spits. Narrow breaches through the barriers enable the ponds to "breathe" with the twice-daily tides. Rich in oysters, quahogs, blue crabs, flounder, bluefish, and scallops, the ponds are being threatened by encroaching development. I saw houses built on stilts right on the spits themselves, waiting for the next hurricane.

Overflying the Thames River just west of Watch Hill, I saw my next destination, the United States Coast Guard Academy spread out over a hundred acres of prime hillside at New London, Connecticut. Chief Lance Jones showed me around the spacious grounds. "The Coast Guard had its roots in the ten revenue cutters commissioned by Secretary of the Treasury Alexander Hamilton in 1790," he told me. "But now it's an armed service of about 38,000 men and women, 250 cutters, and 2,000 smaller boats, helicopters, and planes."

The academy accepts up to 300 freshmen a year, chosen through a nationwide competition. About 10 percent of the new cadets are women. Ensign William Walter of the class of '88 told me: "There were 7,000 applicants the year I joined, and 6,700 were not accepted. The academy is very tough, especially in the beginning. You have to learn how to do what you're told. A whole new environment. By the time we graduated, we had lost about half the class."

Chief Jones and I boarded the cutter *Vigorous* just as Commander A. W. McGrath was inspecting the ship, and out of the blue he invited me along on a cruise. During my two days at sea aboard *Vigorous* my regard for the Coast Guard rose even higher. In smooth weather and, later, during a howling gale, with the ship pitching and rolling, and during fire drills and man-overboard exercises, cool professionalism and good humor reigned.

Executive Officer John Clay told me why he liked the Coast Guard: "You're saving lives, you're fighting drug traffic, you're doing things you can be proud of. So it's a service of proud people. And proud people are happy people. A petty officer may be maintaining buoys one year, chasing drug traffickers the next, cleaning up oil and hazardous-waste spills the year after that, and all the time running around in small boats doing things that would be thought of as adventures by most people." I found myself wondering if the two-billion-dollar annual federal outlay for the Coast Guard might not be the United States government's best bargain.

I drove west along the Connecticut coast as the roadside trees were putting on a brilliant display of glorious fall colors. I paused in Stony Creek, which is trying bravely not to succumb to suburbia. The little town has an air of cheerful abandon. Old Victorian houses painted white, yellow, or gray have a weatherbeaten look as their paint slowly peels. "You can commute to Manhattan from here in an hour and a half," a young man on the town dock told me. Indeed, from here on the air got heavier, and many highway signs pointed toward New York City.

My last stop in New England was at a bridge across a murky tidal creek that separated Byram, Connecticut, from Port Chester, New York—the southern limit of the New England coast. On the bridge two men were fishing but didn't seem to be catching anything. Below them three oily swans were paddling around in the dirty water. The scene held a warning. Without a healthy sea as a partner, New England is unthinkable. The coast, one of the wonders of the world, is too precious to risk.

So, New England, hearken to a heartfelt plea from one old Viking: Take good care of your partner.

*On Mount Desert Island, a quiet
street in Bernard fronts lobster
wharves idled by winter. During this
slow season, scallops supplement
Maine lobstermen's incomes. Spring
brings lobsters to shallow waters and
fills a "lucky trap" for Harry Beal of
Jonesport (below), who displays
market-size specimens.*

PHIL SCHERMEISTER

"A new Prometheus, chained upon the rock / Still grasping in his hand the fire of Jove. . . ," wrote Henry Wadsworth Longfellow, a Maine native, in a tribute to lighthouses. Two centuries after the completion of the Portland Head Light (below) the state's rocky coast remains treacherous to mariners; but summer plantings in Rockport (right) soften the rugged shore's weathered boulders.

Substituting "high touch" for "high tech," students at the Rockport Apprenticeshop (above) establish plank lines for a 19th-century-style Washington County peapod, a small fishing boat. The school, devoted to wooden boatbuilding, emphasizes traditional skills and an earlier era's "pragmatic genius," in the words of director Lance Lee. Sailing for sheer pleasure makes neighboring Camden one of the busiest windjammer ports in the world. Throughout summer its harbor (right) bustles with activity as passengers board schooners for cruises on Penobscot Bay.

Spanking new, a Hinckley Sou'wester 42 undergoes sea trials off Southwest Harbor, Maine. The Mount

Desert Island village boasts half a dozen boat manufacturers legendary in yachting circles.

Rooms with a view flank Brown's Wharf in Boothbay Harbor, a picturesque fishing port as well as one of Maine's most popular summer resorts. Trends and traditions have coexisted peacefully for decades in Boothbay. By contrast, on minuscule Monhegan Island ten miles offshore (right), the near-total absence of modern amenities—cars, bars, streetlights, and street life—provides the allure that swells a year-round population of 80 tenfold in summer.

Double peninsulas shaped like a lobster's claw, Marblehead, Massachusetts, encloses a pleasure-boat

mecca. Summer events draw flotillas; in winter, only hardy "frostbiters" continue sailing.

Business and pleasure mix around Boston's historic waterfront, where sailboats at Lewis Wharf share an

urban panorama with the stately Custom House Tower and new downtown skyscrapers.

Rhythms of sea and sand shape landscapes and life-styles on outer Cape Cod. Along the peninsula's slender forearm (right), the Atlantic slowly erodes and resculpts the high sand cliffs of Cape Cod National Seashore, whose 27,000 acres include ponds, marshes, and woodlands. Here local legend "Wild Bill" Barnum chats with ranger Martha Lyon (below). At the cape's curling tip, Provincetown (above) is home port to an old Portuguese fishing community as well as a newer artists colony.

Gulls dip and wheel above workboats at Menemsha, a working fishing village on Martha's Vineyard.

Visitors buy fresh fish and lobster from the boats, or angle for bonito from nearby jetties.

Precisely spaced umbrellas plant patches of shade at the Cliffside Beach Club on the north shore of Nantucket. Only 12 miles by 6 at its widest, the "Faraway Land"— its Wampanoag name—has 80 miles of beaches and waters warmed by the Gulf Stream. Sky-high real estate values bespeak its low-key appeal, which has seen boom and bust since English settlers purchased it for £30 and two beaver hats in 1659. Whaling ushered in the first golden age; today the cobbled pavements and 19th-century buildings of Nantucket town preserve that legacy (right).

Cottages, Newport style, face Rhode Island Sound near Bailey Beach. At the point, Jefferson Memorial

architect John Russell Pope built a home, The Waves, now divided into condominiums.

Eighty-foot maxiboats go spinnaker-to-spinnaker off Newport in the Swarovski Maxi Series; only a dozen or so of the million-dollar yachts compete worldwide. Newport has a crowded calendar of prestigious yachting events. On a summer day a thicket of masts obscures downtown, where 18th-century Trinity Church (above, at far right) and harborside condos tell of the town's transformation from colonial port to pricey resort. Fishing and lobstering have remained important, though; in Newport Harbor (below), a bumboat offers home delivery to the yachting set.

Built to clear aircraft carriers, Newport Bridge has linked its namesake resort and other Aquidneck

Island communities to the mainland since 1969.

Crisp drills keep tradition alive during a cadet review at the U. S. Coast Guard Academy in New London, Connecticut. White-domed Hamilton Hall honors Alexander Hamilton, who in 1790 founded the Coast Guard's forerunner, the Revenue Cutter Service, to intercept smugglers. Beyond, the Thames River (right), which flows into Long Island Sound, earns respect from sailors—including white-knuckled crew members of a broaching J-boat, awash during intercollegiate races.

Varied ecological threads spin a lacework of marsh and pond, forest and field, freshwater and salt where

the Connecticut River meets the sea about 90 miles from New York City.

III

THE ALLURE OF THE OUT-OF-DOORS

By Tom Melham   Photographs by Phil Schermeister

He came to these woods nearly 150 years ago, a pilgrim seeking necessities he could never find in town: solitude and freedom. Though only a couple of miles south of his birthplace in Concord, Massachusetts—"the oldest inland town in New England," he called it— the woods were a world away in temperament. Here, in a grove of white pines overlooking a small lake, this wiry 28-year-old with the large, sad eyes built a one-room cabin: his home for the next two years. His purpose, he would write later, was "to live deliberately, to front only the essential facts of life, and see if I could not learn what it had to teach and not, when I came to die, discover that I had not lived."

Here he apprenticed himself to the New England outdoors, drinking in its varied moods and seasons. A skilled and introspective observer, he detailed his simple, lakeside life in journals that adroitly plumbed the dimensions of nature's soul— and of his own. "We need the tonic of wilderness," he concluded. "We can never have enough of Nature." Such thoughts ultimately fueled his masterpiece: *Walden*, named for the pond that so inspired him. The man, of course, was Henry David Thoreau; although wilder realms would beckon him, Walden Pond remained Thoreau's turning point, his great departure, and his life's greatest adventure.

Today, 333-acre Walden Pond State Park Reservation memorializes the man and the enduring magic of this bit of outdoor New England. There have been changes since

White birches and sparkling waters welcome canoeists (above) as well as climbers, hikers, fishermen, and other seekers of adventure—or of solitude—to outdoor New England.

Thoreau's 1845-47 stay. A large bathhouse now dominates the pond's eastern shore, where as many as 5,000 bathers flock on a hot summer day. A footpath circles the pond, and trails maze its woods; riprap and retaining walls rein in eroding slopes; and signs implore visitors to stick to trails. Silvery commuter trains thunder past on one side of the preserve; the other side faces Route 126 and a trailer park, adjacent to the Concord town dump. Beset by such intrusions of our century, Thoreau's Walden can seem frail indeed, a casualty of time.

But venture here after summer's crush— as I did one recent October—and you may find that the charms Thoreau celebrated linger. Go to where his cabin stood. Sit upon the forest's slippery, pungent carpet of pine needles and look out on Walden's waters, framed by oaks and maples touched by autumn's fire. The trees still are large, mature, enduring. The terrain still is varied, quickly changing from sandy beaches to wooded hilltops to secluded hollows. From the cabin site you see neither bathhouse nor trailer park nor other works of man; gone are the crowds and noise, replaced by husky creakings and whimpers as breezes bend the pines. A pair of mallards and several sandpipers work the sodden marsh of nearby Wyman Meadow. Though trammeled by too many feet, these woods exude a soothing envelope of solitude, even now. For those who pick their time to visit, Walden lives.

It lives not only in these Concord woods but also in the mountains that make up New England's corrugated spine and in the wooded ridges of the Berkshire Hills. It lives as well on New England's "west coast"—Lake Champlain and its valley— and across the vast, watery North Woods of Maine. It lives in a thousand places throughout New England, where striking physical variety and natural beauty have survived 350 years of human settlement and development. Indeed, this spirit of Walden—this enduring allure of the New England outdoors—goes a long way toward defining the region's very soul.

Lifetime Mainer Randy Cross, adept at numerous backwoods skills, from poling a canoe to trapping and hunting, spends as much time as possible in what he calls "the big woods"—largely the northwestern quadrant of his state. It is Maine's empty quarter, he says. "Nobody lives there any more. From Staceyville up to the Canadian border, it's a blank on the map." Indeed, road maps show few towns and fewer roads across this expanse, in sharp contrast to heavily gridded Quebec Province just next door. Adds Randy with a broad grin and a New England twang, "It's my favorite *paht* of Maine."

I joined Randy and a handful of others one fine spring day to hunt bear—not with rifles or bows, but with a radio. Randy works for the state Department of Inland Fisheries and Wildlife, helping project leader Craig McLaughlin monitor a few of the state's estimated 21,000 black bears. They capture perhaps four dozen animals yearly, tag them, and collar the sows with radio transmitters so they can plot the bears' home ranges and relocate them in later years. Every spring, while mother bears are denned up with their most recent cubs, the men go into Maine's big woods to see how their bears are doing. The search begins by pickup truck cruising low, thickly forested hills toward bear locations determined only days before by aerial radio survey. The truck ride is a chance to quiz Randy on the "black ghost"—his nickname

Alpine boutonniere, a wild rose blooms in a meadow on the flank of Mount Washington in New Hampshire.

for the eastern black bear. "The bears move so quietly," he explains. "They develop specific trails and step in the very same places, time and again. So there's nothing left to crack or snap. All you hear is their breathing—if you're close enough."

He adds, "What most people *think* they know about bears simply is not true. They say, 'Bears stink.' If *you* were to stay put in one place for six months without a toilet or a bath, how do you think you'd smell? A lot worse than a bear. Actually, they have a very weak smell, a sweet smell, not at all unpleasant." Another fallacy, says Randy, is that bears are ferocious. "They don't mean you harm, they don't look for trouble. All they look for is food. I'd rather face a bear than a German shepherd."

One reason, he explains, is that "bears have the best sign language of any animal I know. Dominant bears look you in the eye; others go out of their way to avoid eye contact. It's all intimidation. A bear knows that if he looks directly at you, he's picking a fight. Most don't want to fight, so you can sometimes intimidate them simply by staring them down."

In time, the few roads and near roads we've been chasing no longer head where we need to go. We switch to snowmobiles —stowed in the pickup—and ride them to within a hundred yards or so of a bear site before cutting our engines. Biologist Mark Caron then slings a radio receiver over his

shoulder and grabs earphones and a directional antenna. By slowly rotating the antenna, he can pinpoint the direction of the strongest radio signal—and thus of the bear itself. We pull on snowshoes and set off in single file. The day is warm and sunny, the soft snow rotting beneath an old crust that holds up fairly well under the snowshoes. Sunlight dances through the branches of mixed hardwoods: beech, maple, oak, and ash; mostly beech. Bears love beechnuts, Craig says, though local yields often prove unreliable. Suddenly Mark motions for quiet; we are close to the den. Randy scans the woods and points to a dead fir, partially uprooted and leaning. Such blowdowns, he whispers, "are real typical hideouts. The roots pull up and leave a hollow where the bear can den and feel protected."

Mark's radio soon confirms Randy's suspicion; the fir is indeed the den. But where exactly? Spring's dirty snow uniformly blankets whatever hollows pock the forest floor below. Cautiously we approach, finding a melt hole about six inches across, near the tree. Through it I see black fur. The fur is *moving*, rhythmically, as its owner inhales and exhales. I can't tell what part of the bear I'm seeing.

We plan to anesthetize the sow with a jab stick—a pole ending in a loaded hypodermic needle—then haul it out. But just where it gets its dose has a lot to do with how effective that dose will be. Randy guesses at the bear's position and makes a stab. The black mass doesn't yelp so much as it rustles; Randy covers the den with an old sleeping bag to keep out sun and, he hopes, calm the bear. We wait for the drug to act, listening in vain for the cubs that should be squeaking by now. Disappointment settles on the men. Then Randy hears something, though no one else does, sparking a rash of odds-making that ends with 5 to 2 *against* cubs being present. Two pennies and a nickel—I told you they were researchers—go into a kitty.

Twenty minutes later the bear remains conscious. "It's been too long," says Randy. Too much anesthetic could endanger the animal; too little might endanger us. Craig decides on a half-dose more. Another brief wait, and the test poke engenders no response. We dig out one side of the snow den and wrestle the subdued sow outside, onto the sleeping bag. She is not as large as I expect, weighing 154 pounds, some 25 percent less than I do. Her drugged state makes her seem docile, like a large pet. I've met dogs taller—and a whole lot smellier—than this bear; Randy is absolutely right about the scent.

He and Craig give her what amounts to an annual checkup. They snip hair samples for mineral analysis and inspect teeth for color and condition. They weigh and measure her body, make sure her tags still show, and trade in her old battery-powered radio collar for a new one. Then a glob of eye ointment and a shot of penicillin. I look toward the den and see only a pair of boots—Mark's—jutting from the snow. He has gone headfirst into the den. I urge you not to try this. There is a sharp yowl, and Mark passes back a black, grizzled cub. Then another. A third!

"Each one comes with 20 fishhooks," Randy says, as he puts one on each of my shoulders, the third on my head. "You can't shake 'em off." Their half-inch claws cling like Velcro. They are alert but seem totally relaxed. Remember that they've never been away from mama before, nor have they seen humans—or even daylight! Each weighs between 4 and 5 pounds,

making them about two months old, says Craig. Newborns, he adds, weigh a mere 8 to 12 ounces. Strange that so large a mammal—adult sows can hit 270 pounds—has infants so tiny. Finally one cub begins to squawk. Quickly the three are measured, sexed, tagged, and returned with mother to the den. Craig rebuilds the broken den wall with boughs and snow, piling more snow on top. As we snowshoe out, I can hardly make out the den's location; it's almost as if we had never been there.

To many visitors and residents alike New England is one huge outdoor resource. It's trout fishing or canoeing, skiing or savoring the age-old pleasures of the hunt. It's taking in the fall colors, making a sunset sail, or merely finding a summer retreat from a steaming city. This diversity, coupled with accessibility and compact size—you can drive across New England in under four hours—have made the region a premier playground, certainly the ultimate one for the northeastern megalopolis. For instance, Maine license plates proclaim the state, which fills roughly half of New England, a "vacationland." True enough, yet the nickname presents only one dimension of nature's impact. Many Mainers, and other New Englanders as well, look to the outdoors not only for recreation but also for lifestyles, even livelihoods. Gil Gilpatrick is one.

A registered Maine guide, Gil organizes river trips and teaches snowshoe- and canoe-making as part of a course in outdoor resources in a vocational school. He also writes books, including a spirited history of Maine's Allagash River, which he has canoed perhaps 70 times in more than 20 years of guiding. It's a popular run, part of the National Wild and Scenic Rivers

system, and it brings Gil far more customers than any other river.

"Everyone's heard of the Allagash," he explains, "so they all want to do it. Also, it's one of the easier trips. No big carries, no big rapids. I especially like the variety: lakes, some white water, shifting views of spruce forest in the upper part. Below Allagash Falls it could be a different country—lots of maples, the land more rolling."

The river cleaves Maine's vast, sprawling, and often spongy northwest, densely forested with spruce and fir, dappled with uncountable lakes, and laced with innumerable streams. Indians, says Gil, "traveled virtually everywhere here by canoe. Upstream, downstream—it's a lot easier to canoe upriver than to bushwhack through the woods." Canoes remain the region's ideal craft, for they are lightweight, responsive, of shallow draft yet with ample space for gear and food.

I spent several days canoeing the upper Allagash with Gil and three others, and found it less a river than a series of lakes and ponds interconnected by short streams and portages. The land yawns off in a laminate of thin horizontal layers: flat, brooding waters, pebbly beaches, and wavelike, forested profiles that sweep one upon the other into ever more distant woods. Even the occasional mountains are horizontal, their rounded ridges far longer than tall. The beauty of the Allagash is liquid, always changing yet permanent, like that of the sea. Wildlife abounds.

Merganser families routinely scurry from our approaching canoes, loll about as we catch up, then scurry on again and loll some more. Loons dive and bob and play, full of eerie calls and mysterious ways; a blue heron slowly stalks the farther shore. We see deer and moose nearly every day;

one young bull swims Heron Lake, only his head above water, his ears working like twitchy fan blades as a black haze of flies determinedly sticks to him through heat and high water. Ospreys and bald eagles soar or just cruise the waterway for a meal. Each time we near shore the dense, piney perfume of the forest envelops us—often before we land. Evenings are rich with the varied trumpetings of bullfrog, owl, and loon. One night Churchill Lake is so calm that even the stars clearly reflect in the placid water.

Thoreau rambled some Allagash lakes, traveling mostly by birchbark canoe with Indian guides. Though beset by flies, mud, and contrary winds, he left Maine deeply impressed by his companions' backwoods skills and their closeness to nature—and by the quiet beauty of what he called the area's "stern, yet gentle, wildness."

His words apply even today, though the Allagash is hardly untouched by man. An estimated 12,000 boaters course the waterway annually. Established campsites—complete with tables, fireplaces, and privies—stud the route. Outboard motors are legal, and rangers regularly patrol the waters. Rangers even shuttle boaters' gear around modest Chase Rapids (for a small fee) so the boaters can run the white water unencumbered. In many ways the Allagash is more a cozy outing at grandpa's farm than a wilderness trip.

Still, an illusion of wildness persists, born of the expansive sights, sounds, and moods of the Maine woods. One of my Allagash companions, Maine outdoorsman Gene Lagomarsino, put it this way: "For a lot of people the attraction of the Allagash is that you can come here as an amateur and feel like a pro. You feel you've done something, that you've been through the wilderness—even if it's not wilderness with a capital W."

One morning at six we wake to the growls of a logger's skidder—heavy equipment used to drag felled trees through the woods. Though we cannot see any workers, the noise lasts till sundown. It is a blunt reminder that, although the Allagash Wilderness Waterway is protected from logging, it extends only 500 feet inland from the water's edge. Beyond that narrow band the lands are private, and trees may be cut—though, within a mile, only with the Waterway's permission. Most of the forested views we've seen actually have been *outside* the preserve. And although Maine's northwest may seem a huge, roadless blank on the map, it actually is crisscrossed with the logging roads of paper companies, which have owned and harvested this area for more than a century.

Hints of wildness echo throughout the New England landscape, even in some popular and heavily used areas. New Hampshire's craggy White Mountains, for example, draw recreationists every season of the year. Primary magnet is 6,288-foot Mount Washington, highest point in New England—and notorious home of the country's worst weather. Winds in 1934 gusted to 231 miles an hour on the summit, setting a world record that still stands.

One sunny October day in 1988 four Boston fraternity brothers eager for fall colors set their sights on Mount Washington. They began hiking around noon, admittedly late, but they'd climbed Mount Washington before and figured that as long as they made the top by sunset they could hitch a ride down the mountain's auto road. They carried one pack but no heavy clothing. After an hour and a half one of the four turned back, deciding his boots weren't up to the outing. The others continued, making the halfway point around 4:30. By then, fog, rising winds, and even snow flurries were beginning to challenge them and their marginal clothing. It was getting late, too.

"But we wanted to go all the way," recalled hiker Steve Sardella. The three reassured themselves, reasoning that they could always turn back. Lacking camping gear, they certainly didn't intend to stay the night.

But they didn't turn back, though winds gusted to 30, 50, then 70 miles an hour; though thickening snows obscured the trail ahead and erased their footprints behind. "It got worse and worse," Sardella told me. Foolhardy but determined, they made the summit—by then a howling wilderness of white. They searched in vain for the auto road. They didn't know it had been closed all day; even if they'd found it there would have been no cars to flag down. Steve saw a sign to Lakes of the Clouds Hut. "We went off 15 or 20 yards, couldn't see anything, went another 20 yards. Then we were *really* lost." They didn't realize they'd crossed over to the mountain's far side. Suddenly they were wallowing in chin-deep drifts among thickets of scrub spruce. Visibility plunged to ten feet. The group's oldest hiker, 23-year-old Andrew Stewart, got so cold that for a time he couldn't move his legs. "I thought it was all over," he later confided. Somehow the trio kept on, hoping to blunder onto a trail before daylight faded completely. They didn't find one.

They did, however, come to a creek, which led to a clearing. And there, thanks to some dollar bills and other bits of paper gleaned from wallets, they coaxed damp twigs and other kindling to ignite. All night they fed the fire, talking to keep up spirits as temperatures plummeted; the summit recorded a windchill of 17 degrees below zero. Says Steve, "It was pretty scary. It happened so fast, the wind coming up, the snow. I never knew you could be so alone in New England."

With dawn's gray light, the battered hikers continued down the creek, eventually reaching a trail and, finally, a highway. They emerged exhausted, embarrassed, and euphoric; they had survived.

Their ascent traced Tuckerman's Ravine, a glacier-carved hanging valley on Mount Washington's southern shoulder. Tuckerman's *collects* snow—so much that skiers come here as late as May or even June, months after nearby peaks turn bare. They struggle and sweat, taking half a day to lug skis, boots, poles, and themselves up the ravine—all for a single ten-minute descent. As many as 2,000 have done it on the same day. Still, they constitute but a tiny fraction of New Hampshire's ski community.

In New England nature's ties are economic as well as aesthetic; the region boasts a huge outdoor-oriented industry that includes ski corporations, yacht clubs, myriad guides and outfitters and charters, resort hotels, country inns and backwoods camps, a cornucopia of tour and travel services, and numerous manufacturers of outdoor gear. L. L. Bean built its reputation on hunting shoes, then broadened into a supermarket for casual clothing as well as camping and outfitting items.

Old Town Canoes (made in Old Town, Maine) and Mad River Canoes (of Waitsfield, Vermont) also are known worldwide. Though smaller and newer, Burton Snowboards in Vermont has gained coast-to-coast fame manufacturing a cross between a surfboard and a ski that is designed for surfing down snowy slopes. These and hundreds of other recreation-related concerns in New England contribute to an industry so complex and diverse that a tally of its size is impossible.

Henri Vaillancourt of Greenville, New Hampshire, in the state's south, plays a role in this industry, though L. L. Bean hardly feels threatened. This descendant of French-Canadian immigrants makes canoes: *birchbark* canoes. Only a handful of people share his craft. Henri taught himself, starting some 25 years ago. "A birchbark canoe is a very romantic thing," Henri said, adding that as a boy he developed a boyish interest in the first New Englanders, the Penobscot and Malecite and Algonquin Indians. It was no passing fancy. To him the bark canoe was the epitome of Indian craft and lore; making one became his goal. After reading what little he could find on the subject, he built his first—at age 14. "It wasn't very good. But it floated."

Henri enjoys the canoe's simple design: "Essentially it's a big bark bag stuffed with ribs. The ribs push the bark out to the desired shape; pressure holds everything together. It's pretty ingenious construction."

He told me all this while hunched on the lawn before his house, shaping what would become the gunwales of his next canoe—entirely by eye. No plans, no forms, no complicated tools. Only an idea of how the finished piece should look and a crooked knife, an age-old tool traditional to the northern U.S. and Canada and almost totally unknown elsewhere. Henri makes his own with six-inch handles and four-inch blades fashioned from old files. The blade may be straight or curved, but the handle is always crooked, for it is meant to fit across the palm and project to the out-stretched thumb. It is pulled toward the body, not pushed away as in whittling, giving far better control and more power with each stroke. It is a fast, versatile, and accurate tool.

Henri, whose short blond hair, crinkly face, and ready smile recall the young Paul Newman, gathers all raw materials for his canoes himself, directly from the woods: bark of paper birch, white cedar for frame and ribs, spruce roots for lashings. No lumberyard stocks these items, not even the cedar, which must be hand-split. Sawed wood, Henri explains, not only is nontraditional but also is inherently weak, because sawing ignores the way a tree grows, cutting across the grain and producing wood likely to crack. Splitting, however, *follows* the grain, yielding wood that is very strong for its weight. But because split wood follows the grain, Henri needs exceptionally straight-grained trees—and so he selects them himself, at times traveling a thousand miles to find the right ones. He enjoys these jaunts for wood and bark, striving to get a single piece of bark for each canoe. "It's part of the romance. You go into the woods, and the trees are standing nice and tall and clean. It feels good, more satisfying than buying something in a store."

Eventually he returns to his lawn, splits the cedar into strips, unrolls the bark and the spruce roots, sits down with his crooked knife, and simply commences making another canoe.

"I like long, flowing curves, nothing hard," he says. So, apparently, do his customers. There is a two-year waiting list for would-be owners of Vaillancourt canoes, who pay up front. The price: four hundred dollars per linear foot, or six or seven thousand dollars each. Henri says that most

buyers use their purchases, though few risk them in white water. Some canoes go to collectors and never get wet. Currently he builds three or four a year, leaving time for skiing or visiting Indian friends in northern Quebec and for making snowshoes and crooked knives. "Recreation and work have been very much entwined in my life," he muses. Does he envision himself on the lawn 20 years from now, still turning out bark canoes?

"I certainly hope so," he grins.

On New England's "west coast" Lake Champlain beckons from between the beautiful, corrugated walls of New York's Adirondacks and Vermont's Green Mountains. The novelist Henry James once wrote that Champlain "strikes you more as a river" than a lake, since its length (107 miles) so dwarfs its width (12 miles at its widest).

Together with the Hudson River, Champlain is a moat that severs New England and a sliver of New York from the rest of the country. Historically the lake has been the region's primary avenue. Indian tribes relied on it, British armies used it to attack and evict French forces from the continent and then tried to cleave the rebellious American colonies along the natural valley.

Today Champlain serves as one of New England's boating meccas, drawing everything from luxury cruisers to windsurfers and yachts, including *Intrepid*, two-time winner of the America's Cup. Burlington—Vermont's biggest city and Champlain's chief metropolis—is a fast growing area. Yet one still can experience a mountain climber's solitude and sense of discovery even here, a mere hundred feet from Burlington's breakwater. The trick is to go 40 feet *down*, using scuba gear to plumb a

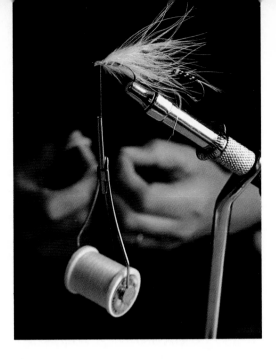

Nimble fingers tie a black ghost fly. Its peacock-feather streamers will pulsate underwater to attract salmon and lake trout, both plentiful in New England.

realm devoid of bustle, devoid of crowds, devoid of most sounds.

Diving in Lake Champlain? This is no balmy, coral-reefed paradise; its waters are often frigid and murky. But there *are* reasons to take the plunge. Start at a mooring buoy near the breakwater. Its chain leads down through darkening waters that may offer only 15 feet of visibility. You drop slowly, catching sight of the barred sides of lake perch—up to 18 inches long—which have learned to seek handouts from divers. You near the bottom but stay above it, so as not to roil the fine silt that can cut visibility to zero. A yellow guideline runs along the lake floor, and you follow it. Suddenly a hulk looms from the gray murk like a vision out of delirium. It is a wooden ship, the *General Butler*, victim of a December gale more than a century ago. It is oddly intact. Iron fittings, rusty but still sound, bolster the solid wood deck and hull. Hand-carved wooden deadeyes and cleats stand out perfectly intact. The boat is 14 feet wide—narrow enough for canals—and 88 feet long, clumsy looking but innovative in that it fulfilled two very different tasks. The *Butler* was a sailing canal boat. Two masts and a centerboard enabled it to sail Lake Champlain; lowering its masts and raising the centerboard permitted it to enter Champlain Canal, which connected the lake to the Hudson River.

You glide sternward over *Butler's* deck, pausing to peer through open hatches into the hold, where marble blocks once bound for Burlington still sit amid wood and iron struts that reinforce the hull. The centerboard—in the up position—fills the centerboard trunk. Perhaps the impact of hitting bottom shoved it there, though the captain may have hauled it in when he tried to keep his doomed ship off the breakwater.

Continuing aft you see the remains of the steering mechanism, which broke during *Butler's* approach to Burlington Harbor. The captain's makeshift repair—lashing a tiller to the damaged post—tells of the drama of those final moments. Cracks in *Butler's* bow testify to multiple collisions with the breakwater, each impact allowing one of the people on board to leap to safety. Though the cracks made the ship swamp and sink, no large holes pierce the hull or deck. The entire ship remains remarkably sound—especially when you consider that it went down in 1876.

Dave Skinas, a diver and survey archaeologist with Vermont's Division for Historic Preservation, explains: "The lake's cold, fresh water makes for excellent preservation; it's like seeing ships when they first went down." In the ocean, iron turns to rusty encrustations, often in just a few years, and worms and other organisms reduce wood boats to mush. Champlain is free of such organisms, and its oxygen-poor bottom makes a near-ideal repository for wrecks, creating what local diver Bill Everest calls "an underwater museum."

Then, too, Champlain has had its share of sinkings. It is, in fact, America's most historic body of water, strategically important from colonial times through the War of 1812. Benedict Arnold launched a hastily built fleet that battled the Royal Navy here during the American Revolution, winning time for George Washington's bedraggled army. In addition to wartime casualties, a rich history of boatbuilding and commercial shipping have endowed this lake with diverse wrecks. How many?

"Easily a hundred—probably closer to two hundred," says local maritime historian Art Cohn. He considers Champlain to have "the richest collection of inland wooden American ships anywhere. From before the Revolution through the age of commercial wood boats." In addition to *General Butler* and the remains of Arnold's fleet, Champlain boasts *Phoenix I*—history's oldest existing steamer hull, sunk in 1819—and a horse-powered paddle-wheel ferry that is the only known example of its kind in the world. But, says Cohn, "perhaps only a third of the wrecks have been inventoried, and fewer than 20 have been closely studied. That's why it's so important to preserve what we have here."

In 1985 Vermont initiated a system of underwater preserves meant to encourage recreational divers to visit and help protect designated wrecks. So far three preserves have been set aside, with others planned. The hope is to prevent vandalism and accidental destruction of these resources by publicizing their existence and by instilling local pride.

Vermonters call their home the Green Mountain State, and within sight of Lake Champlain the mountains rise. More tapered and flowing than New Hampshire's White Mountains, the Greens are the older formation, born of ancient geologic collisions between North America and Africa. Once they stood perhaps twice their present height. Their parallel ridges run roughly north and south, virtually fill-

ing Vermont and extending through western Massachusetts as the Berkshire Hills.

The Berkshires summon up cultural and rural charms far more than woodland wilds. But even in this most civilized bastion, surprises occur. I especially recall one southbound road here; the asphalt surface soon turned to dirt, then to a single lane. I expected it to peter out or dead-end any minute. But it led on and on, through thickly wooded hills, with leafy branches meeting overhead in an unbroken bower of fall colors. The golden leaves, combined with sunlight equally golden, shot the land through with warmth. I left my car to ramble the unbroken forest, where its solid canopy had kept the floor largely unencumbered by brush. Ground cover included ferns, mosses, mountain laurel, and rhododendron. Clumps of bracken ran the spectrum from greens through yellows and golds to burnt copper. Leaves had begun to fall, splashing the floor with color. The pungent scent of tannin filled the air with the odor of damp earth and decaying leaves, of thriving ferns and rotting, moss-covered blowdowns.

These woods turn out to be fairly new, a feral wilderness born of lands tamed and later abandoned. Such reclaimed wilds spatter much of New England, which is far more wooded now than it was a century ago. By the mid-1800s, Connecticut and Vermont were three-quarters cleared; today they are nearly three-quarters *forested*, while Maine's woods cover some 90 percent of that state. Largely these comebacks resulted not from reforestation projects but from natural forces. Glaciers left much of New England's soil thin and rocky, and once colonists felled the virgin forest many farms proved marginal at best. Owners left for factories or homesteads in the far more

Twin blossoms of bunchberry, a low-growing herb, brighten a White Mountain notch, or deep valley.

fertile Midwest. Gradually the trees re-turned—for New England's forests are not as fragile as tropical ones. They possess a feisty ability to regenerate themselves and their soil even after multiple cuttings.

In addition to feral woods, the Berk-shires harbor dozens of relic wilds: places like Bashbish Falls, a sinuous cataract that bursts from a bouldered, plunging ridge on the Massachusetts–New York border to feed a chuckling trout stream; or the Ice Glen near Stockbridge, a ravine jumbled with dramatic glacial debris and studded with giant hemlocks that are between two and three centuries old. Both are relatively small bits of nature that for one reason or another have escaped man's heavy hand.

Another relic is Bartholomew's Cobble, in Ashley Falls, Massachusetts. Named for former owner George Bartholomew, this rocky knoll, or cobble, rises like a mini-mountain from the floodplain of the Hou-satonic River. Its marble and quartzite date back half a billion years; it has resisted gla-ciers, geologic upheavals, even man. Time has fractured it with sheer drops, crags, ra-vines, caves, and Swiss-cheese solution holes leached by acids in the soil. Each fis-sure creates its own microenvironment, giving rise to remarkably diverse vegeta-tion. Hemlocks cling to bare outcrops, their roots veining the rock and seemingly squeezing nutrients from it. Other trees— such as cottonwoods—prefer more fertile hollows; one giant measures six feet across.

The cobble's main attractions, however, tend to the Lilliputian. Wispy mosses and dwarf ferns, sundews and spleenworts, and a palette of wildflowers, all fringe its crevices and ledges, lending an enchanted feel to this pocket wilderness. Each bend and niche holds yet another surprise, wild grapes or wild ginger, some new shape or shade or scent. More spartan inhabitants grace the dry western face: lichens rather than mosses or ferns, barberry and cedar instead of maple and pine.

The reserve that encompasses the knoll is small—a rumpled fairyland of just 277 acres—yet it nurtures some 800 plant spe-cies, including 53 fernlike varieties.

Editor, educator, and frequent cobble visitor Mark Van Doren summed up the ar-ea's magic as "an experience that cannot be had elsewhere in this part of the world and at this turn of time. Bartholomew's Cobble is an oasis in the wilderness that modern man is making: a small but precious emi-nence, a little marble mountain upon whose sides grow trees of ancient origin and plants of unimaginable age. May noth-ing ever threaten its serenity."

His words are reminiscent of Thoreau; they hang on the wall of a cabin not much larger than Thoreau's, one stuffed with natural history displays beside the cobble. The Trustees of Reservations—a Massa-chusetts corporation established to set aside certain natural sites for public use— administers the tract that includes the cab-in and Bartholomew's Cobble, which also ranks as a National Natural Landmark. Like Bashbish Falls or Ice Glen or even Wal-den Pond, the cobble pays tribute to the na-ture of New England. This region's outdoors remains diverse, resilient, and enduring—in spite of man's long presence here. And perhaps because of it.

Leaning into the hill, skiers trace graceful turns on Mount Mansfield, at 4,393 feet Vermont's highest peak. Near the base lies Stowe, a resort sometimes called the ski capital of the East. An average of 225 inches of snow falls on the state of Vermont each winter, blanketing 25 alpine centers and approximately 1,200 miles of acclaimed ski trails.

Rocky grandeur of New Hampshire's Presidential Range, the backbone of New England, challenges

hikers. These ponder their goal—6,288-foot Mount Washington, New England's highest mountain.

Cool nerves and cold-weather gear help a climber (above) scale icy Frankenstein Cliffs in Crawford Notch State Park, a retreat cupped in the White Mountains of New Hampshire. An ice ax and sharp-spiked crampons pin him to the slippery wall; his Gore-tex bib overalls repel wind and water, and gaiters keep snow out of his boots. Nearby, on less precarious footing, cross-country skiers share a drink from the frosty Ellis River.

Kayakers and canoeists tense for the start of an 18-mile race on the Connecticut River in New

Hampshire. Bark canoes crafted by Indians from the region's birch trees once plied these waters.

Waders, floaters, and boaters share the shallows of Sandbar State Park (above), an offshore preserve in Lake Champlain near Burlington, Vermont. Not far away at North Beach, triathlon contestants finish a mile swim (right). Still ahead: a 25-mile bicycle race and a 6-mile run. Lake Champlain's 107-mile length defines more than half of Vermont's western border; it also compensates Vermonters—the only landlocked New Englanders—for their lack of an Atlantic seacoast.

Blustery winds tauten spinnakers on Lake Champlain. A two-man day sailer hurries from harm's way

as racing yachts approach a turn buoy.

"Rock climbing is like dancing," says Joe Lentini (right), director of a New Hampshire climbing school. "You must know where to put your feet and how to balance your weight over them." As his partner, Pat Wespiser, belays him, Joe inches up a route on White Horse Ledge called Inferno, a 600-foot climb in the White Mountains. At the top, his view will include the backside of another popular cliff—Cathedral Ledge (below), which faces the distant Saco River.

Hiker Mark Hitchcock maps his next steps on the Appalachian Trail at Lakes of the Clouds Hut in the White Mountains. The A. T., a national scenic trail that winds 2,100 miles between Georgia and Maine, takes the high, scenic route through five of the New England states. In Maine, Screw Auger Falls (right) tempts A. T. hikers down a short side trail in Grafton Notch State Park.

Ghostly spires in morning mist, pines rise in Maine's fabled North Woods (above). Paper companies own nearly six million acres of softwoods here; visitors pay a fee and enter through checkpoints. Once in, they dodge hurtling trucks, which carry up to 200,000 pounds of logs.

Rugged splendor of northern Maine spreads beyond a bouldered ridge atop Katahdin, a granite monolith

in Baxter State Park. The 5,267-foot peak anchors the northern end of the Appalachian Trail.

Washboard of white water, New Hampshire's Indian Creek rolls toward fly-fisherman Layford Collins. Numerous rivers and lesser streams nurture New England's love affair with water sports. Rafters (below) taste the fury of the Cribworks, a hair-raising set of rapids on Maine's Penobscot River.

In Baxter Park a moose calf shadows its mother during a mealtime browse for aquatic plants. Baxter encompasses 314 square miles of mountains and forest, the gift of former governor Percival Baxter. Though remote, the park requires reservations for its campsites during its May to October season to avoid overcrowding, especially in the popular south; farther north, such backcountry hideaways as Pogy Pond (below) often pass the day in perfect solitude.

Sky-painted waters of a pond near Ossipee, New Hampshire, shimmering with evergreens and

birches, reflect the traditional attractions of autumn in New England.

IV

THE CITIES
AND
THE ARTS

By Cynthia Russ Ramsay   Photographs by Nicholas DeVore III

I hadn't been long in New England before I discovered some remarkable facts, ingredients in the high-voltage amalgam of talent, intellect, and enterprise that make that region such a dynamic, fascinating place.

Consider: There are 264 colleges and universities in New England—an extraordinary concentration in an area smaller than the state of Missouri; banks in Boston manage more than 420 billion dollars in assets, making the city the leading financial center of the nation, after New York City; New England has more physicians per capita than any other region, and also the highest per capita income; the Massachusetts legislature appropriates more money per person for arts agencies than any state except Alaska. The country's first public school,

Boston Latin, opened its doors in 1635, and four years later a printing press was assembled across the river in Cambridge.

In Connecticut—where, incidentally, the lollipop, the corkscrew, and the steamboat were invented—insurance companies protect much of the country's businesses, and theaters have stolen some of the limelight from Broadway. Computers, radar, and the guidance systems used in space travel were conceived at MIT—the Massachusetts Institute of Technology—in Cambridge, a

Long a citadel of finance and culture and more recently a hub of high-tech industry, Boston has enjoyed an era of prosperity that included a downtown building boom. A commuter (above) checks the market while waiting for his train.

community also home to Harvard University. Writer Bret Harte supposedly said that it was impossible to fire off a revolver there without bringing down the author of a two-volume work.

Perhaps nowhere else in America would I find such productive people with such a passion for the arts. Where else but in the Berkshire Hills of Massachusetts could I hear superstar conductor and composer Leonard Bernstein and the director of the Boston Symphony, Seiji Ozawa, rehearsing within 1,500 feet of each other. Few private libraries can match the genteel ambience of the Boston Athenaeum, with its long, vaulted reading room resplendent with Oriental rugs, superb sculptures, antique furniture, and large vases of fresh flowers. And few cities of 60,000 have as many fine paintings, as many beautiful old buildings, and such a flourishing symphony, string quartet, and choral society as Portland, Maine.

It's difficult to convey the rich cultural life in New England—the sheer abundance of art treasures, the avalanche of music, and the variety of performances. And add to that mix the heady boomtown environment—where fortunes are being made—and the charm of cities, where graceful old buildings of marble, wood, or brick mellow the strident arrogance of glass and steel.

In the 18th century Yankee merchants grew rich on the trade in rum, slaves, and molasses. Later they prospered in whaling, in the China trade, and in the mills they built along the rivers. Writing in *The Economy of Cities,* Jane Jacobs points out that in the 19th century New England industries produced the textiles that clothed the country, the textbooks that educated its young, the guns that armed its troops, and the tools that cleared the forests and broke the prairie sod. Some of the enormous profits went into the construction of rows of patrician brick townhouses with ornate doorways and wrought-iron balconies on Beacon Hill, once the address of the most proper Bostonians.

As I strolled this still fashionable neighborhood the gas street lamps cast arcs of amber clarity in the chill autumn dusk. Leaves descended like golden snowflakes and eddied across the brick pavement. At one of the long windows that faced Louisburg Square, a girl with hair in long braids played a grand piano—a cameo of privileged childhood in a rectangle of light.

On Charles Street the shops were stylishly quaint. Even the hardware store was lit by chandeliers. One shop specialized in antique doorknobs, another in Italian ice creams; books were sold with a whisper-soft Bach fugue playing in the background.

My destination was the exclusive Somerset Club, a lingering bastion of the aloof and aristocratic Boston Brahmins. Well-heeled and well-educated, these heirs of the merchant princes used their inherited wealth to patronize literature, the arts, and institutions of higher learning. In their heyday in the 19th century they made Boston the country's capital of culture. The city came to be known as the Athens of America, where such heroes of American letters as Hawthorne, Emerson, Alcott, and John Greenleaf Whittier convened, and high-minded gentlemen, freed from the pressures of earning a living, founded such organizations as the American Ornithological Union, the Horticultural Society, the Society for Impecunious Ladies of Gentle Birth, and the Boston Symphony Orchestra.

For S. Parkman Shaw, Jr., descendant of

the old guard and head of the Somerset Club's membership committee, a person's ethical and social values are what count. "I'm wary of those who have become instantly successful. They are in such a hurry they overlook the quality of their lives. I doubt many of them would know how to behave here," he said, as we talked in one of the club's high-ceilinged sitting rooms.

Shaw has been involved in fund-raising for Harvard and for Groton, the distinguished boarding school in Massachusetts. He dines regularly at the club, enjoying, he says, "the amiable conversation that comes from the friction of friendly minds. We may be a group of static, downwardly mobile people, but unlike the so-called movers and shakers, our reputations do not hang on the amount of money we make."

"First we lost political control of the city to the Irish. They ran the city, while we ran the banks. Then over the last 25 years we've also lost most of the financial control." After reflecting for a moment Shaw leaned forward with a glint in his Yankee blue eyes and murmured, "But in spite of their wealth and power, what those new people want is to be like us here—to see themselves as secure in their social standing as in their bank accounts."

Newcomers have taken over other parts of the city as well. A survey in 1988 showed that nearly one third of Boston's heads of households have lived in the city five years or less, and almost half had arrived within the past decade.

Most stable of all the neighborhoods, and the most close-knit, is South Boston—the relentlessly Irish part of town. Places like the Keltic Korner Food Store and St. Bridget's Church announce the area's identity. From "pill hill," where doctors once had their offices in their brick homes, to streets lined with South Boston's typical wood-frame, three-story apartment buildings—called triple deckers—people come up to shake hands with William "Billy" Bulger, who greets them all by name. First elected to the legislature in 1960, Bulger is President of the Massachusetts Senate and a formidable but controversial power in state politics. With him my tour of Southie turned into an entertaining mix of local lore and anecdotes about James Michael Curley, the legendary Irish political boss.

Rascal and Robin Hood in cutaway coat and silk top hat, Curley ran campaigns reviling the Yankee establishment. He was elected mayor of Boston and member of Congress four times and governor once. From 1900 to 1956 Curley commanded the loyalty of Boston's immigrant poor; they overlooked the excesses and misdeeds that sent him to prison twice, taking pride in the poor Irish boy who made good.

"He built schools, playgrounds, and parks for them, regardless of cost, and paid for it by playing games with the tax rate for the rich Yankees," said Bulger. "On one occasion, when the Yankee bankers wanted to raise the interest on a loan to the city, Curley threatened to swamp the bank basements by opening the floodgates in the sewers." Like Curley, Bulger sees himself as the upstart Irishman protecting the interests of the urban poor—finding people jobs and rehabilitating low-income housing projects, such as the one he once called home. He makes no apology for his opposition to forced school busing in the 1970s, an issue that once wracked the city with racial violence. "Any child should be able to go to any school, whatever his color. But he must also be allowed to stay in his neighborhood if he wants. It was the uprooting against parental wish that I opposed," said Bulger adamantly. "Sociologists now recognize the importance of neighborhoods in giving people a sense of identity amidst the anonymity of the big city."

For Bulger, as for his boyhood hero, politics is the greatest game on earth. Yet Bulger is not a mere throwback. Well-read and urbane, he lives simply in a comfortable house in South Boston with his wife and nine children. And it is a measure of the changes taking place in Boston that Billy is a member of the Board of Overseers of that most Brahmin of institutions, the Boston Symphony, and is a trustee of the venerable Boston Public Library.

"These days even some Italians sit on the board of directors of important organizations, and a black is the chairman of the Boston Opera Company," said Lawrence S. DiCara, a high-powered attorney proud of his Italian heritage and enthusiastic about his hometown.

"Boston is not so big that it's unmanageable. If someone is unhappy about a pothole or a developer's plan to build a high rise, he can do something about it. Downtown is also small enough that you can easily get around on foot. And the narrow streets, which were cow paths in their day, bring you face to face with history. Seeing these lovely old buildings affects the way I think. Boston has a great location, too," he added. "You can be in a quiet place in the mountains or by the sea in less time than lots of people elsewhere take to commute.

"And then there are the Red Sox," said DiCara, getting up to swing one of the baseball bats he displays in his office. He called my attention to a statue of Ted Williams on the shelf. "He was the great cult figure of my youth."

New Englanders are nuts about their professional baseball team; a 1986 Nobel prizewinner showed up for his press conference wearing a Red Sox cap. DiCara stoutly maintains there's no stadium like Fenway Park. "All the grass is real—not like those places they carpet with artificial turf, which, in my opinion, is a mortal sin." Rabid sports fans also root for New England's four other professional teams—basketball's Celtics, ice hockey's Bruins and Whalers, and football's Patriots.

Boston's boom, which began in the late 1960s, has added 27 skyscrapers to the city in the past decade and revitalized downtown. One of the most successful projects transformed a rundown produce and meat market into the festive Faneuil Hall Marketplace. More than a million people a month flock to its dozens of boutiques, restaurants, and food stalls. Named for the historic town hall near the entrance, the mall reflects the amiable Boston juxtaposition of old and new. You can sit on a bench eating an egg roll just steps from the sedate building where patriots of the Revolution assembled to protest British rule.

In the flower market pumpkins were on display, but the weather was still warm enough for a juggler and magician to wow

the cheerful crowds in the open-air promenade. The fleet of pushcarts was also out in full force selling jewelry, sweaters, and oversize cookies.

I managed to keep my appetite intact, saving it for one of the *ristorantes* in the North End, Boston's Little Italy and oldest neighborhood. These days food has become the focal point for most visitors to the North End, and I joined the hungry parade peering into the array of restaurants—60 at one count. We were trying to decide on a place to eat. Some restaurants had gilt-edged mirrors, paintings on their ceilings, and waiters in tuxedos; others dished out pasta in home-style eateries that seated 18, with decor consisting of paper napkins and a map of Italy on the wall. My choice was a cafe where locals gather, and I could drink a frothy cappuccino and listen to the lyrical sounds of Italian embellished with effusive gestures of hands.

Traditionally Boston has been a city of neighborhoods—with the same people living in the same houses for generations. In the North End, once almost 100 percent Italian, newcomers now make up about half the population. The warren of narrow, twisting streets so close to the waterfront appeals to young professionals, who like its raffish, gregarious charm and the convenience to downtown. Grandmothers in black shawls still gossip on the front steps; men still gather on Sunday to watch the rebroadcast of soccer games from Italy; laundry still flutters on clotheslines. But these vignettes from an earlier time are disappearing. Even the Prince Spaghetti Factory has been converted into expensive condos. And as the influx of newcomers drives prices up, yuppies displace the working class, and the old tenements sprout flower boxes in the windows instead of wash.

The going rates for real estate are even higher on the elegant, tree-canopied boulevards of the Back Bay, where many of the elaborate Victorian mansions and brownstones are occupied by upscale shops, art galleries, and apartments for the young, single, and affluent new Bostonians.

From all over America, impressive intellects are drawn to the Boston area. Each year well over 200,000 students swarm to this intellectual mecca, home to 60 degree-granting institutions, most notably Harvard and MIT, the formidable titans of academia. Many graduates remain in the area and go on to pursue careers in education, science, medicine, and industry.

Boston also has a reputation as a city of music. You sense the extent of this by looking at the impressive listings in Thursday's Calendar section of the Boston *Globe*. One weekend in October the medley of sounds included jazz and hard rock, choral music of the Ukraine, a balladeer from Scotland, computer-generated music, and more than 30 concerts of classical works.

A perennial favorite is the Boston Symphony Orchestra, one of the country's most revered cultural institutions. So loyal is its following that many of the best seats for its concerts have been passed down as family heirlooms. Summer brings a special offering—free concerts by the Boston Pops on the Esplanade along the Charles River.

Also exceptional has been the collaboration of science and money in the Boston area. Along Route 128, which arcs around the city's western suburbs, and in the glossy new high rises around MIT, smart investors joined forces with the best brains in high technology to found companies that turned new discoveries into profits. The products—calculators, word processors, pacemakers, minicomputers, solar energy devices—have contributed mightily to the modern age. A number of new enterprises hitched their wagons to such futuristic stars as genetic engineering and a new breed of clever computers that can read handwriting and take dictation.

A key ingredient in these endeavors was MIT, a scientific powerhouse across the Charles River that has launched countless partnerships with industry. A thousand faculty members—including eight Nobel Prize winners—and some 2,300 full-time researchers spend their days delving into mysteries ranging from subatomic quarks to genetic links with cancer.

About a mile away is Harvard Square, a carnival of street musicians, hippies, preppies, punks, Rastafarians, and assorted chess players, pipe smokers, and bookworms. Untroubled by it all are the residents of the quiet, leafy streets nearby. They wear bow ties and tweed jackets or skirts and sensible shoes and are apt to be found at plays, poetry readings, lectures, or lobbying for national or local causes. Most of all, these Cantabrigians read books. And just about any kind is available in Cambridge's 26 bookstores—more per square mile than anywhere else in the U.S.

The love affair with the printed page is of long duration. English novelist Arnold Bennet, who arrived in Boston in 1911, wrote: "When I got to the entirely admirable hotel, I found a book in a prominent situation on the writing table in my room. In many hotels this book would have been the Bible. But here it was the catalogue of the hotel library; it ran to 182 pages. On the other hand, there was no bar in the hotel, and no smoking room."

From its earliest beginnings New England has nurtured a deep respect for the written word and intellectual achievement. This commitment owes its origins to Puritan doctrines, which placed a premium on education in the quest for salvation and for status in society. Only five years after the Puritans came ashore their children were attending the Boston Latin School under schoolmaster Philemon Pormont. It is still one of the country's finest public schools.

Academic excellence has brought fame to Phillips Exeter Academy in Exeter, New Hampshire, one of the dozen or so preparatory schools for which New England is well known. Coeducational since 1970, with students from almost every state and from many foreign countries, Exeter still is guided by the principles set forth in its constitution in 1782. In the belief that "goodness without knowledge is weak and feeble, yet knowledge without goodness is dangerous," the goal of the school remains to build character and train minds for "usefulness to mankind."

Nothing conveys the quality of Exeter's education like spending time in class. I might have chosen to attend one on Multivariable Calculus, Chinese Literature, or Existentialism, but I decided on a course in the history department called Capitalism and its Critics. As I walked across the spacious campus the bell in the clock tower sounded the start of class. Everett Arthur Gilcreast, B.A., M.A., Ph.D. from Yale, had already begun the day's discussion with his students—just ten of them, seated with him around a table. He put searching and provocative questions based on the homework assignment to one student, then another. In between there was lively debate and little chance for a student who was unprepared to slip by undetected.

"But these youngsters like to study. They take learning seriously," Dr. Gilcreast told me later. "This is a place where it is fashionable to do homework. What distinguishes us from other schools are the students. Only one out of three who apply is admitted, so we really do take the highly motivated and the very best."

While Exeter nurtures young minds, the MacDowell Colony in Peterborough, some 50 miles to the west, provides artists a retreat that caters to their needs and comforts and secludes them from the distractions of daily life. No telephones ring; no chores take up time; there's no need to figure out what's for dinner. Thornton Wilder, who wrote *Our Town* in one of the studios scattered through the 450 wooded acres, wrote of the colony: "How I needed it, needed to hear myself think and to get out of all this tumult . . . in which there was no chance, really, to explore oneself." Among the more than 3,000 artists who have spent time here since its founding in 1907 are composer Aaron Copland, cartoonist Jules Feiffer, poet Stephen Vincent Benét, and novelists Willa Cather and James Baldwin.

I met some of the current residents as they relaxed before dinner. "We have a lot of steam worked up from being alone all day, so we're eager to talk," said Doris Vila, a slender, intense young artist who works with light as her medium. She uses combinations of lasers, mirrors, theater lights, projections, holograms, and sculptures to bring about environmental creations that may be 1,200 feet square. Doris spoke of the fellowship among MacDowell residents, who are all going through the same struggles with the creative process and facing the same challenges, whether a blank piece of paper or an empty canvas.

When I left the artists to their dinner it was still light enough to see the loveliness of the autumn trees flaming at the edge of the overcast, slate sky. There was also time to stop in Manchester, New Hampshire's largest city. My appointment was with Dean Kamen, inventor, developer, and captain of industry; and my destination was not one of the city's new glass towers but the old Amoskeag Mill, which was once the largest textile operation in the world. When it shut down on Christmas Eve of 1935, 15,000 people lost their jobs.

"From my helicopter, the long, crumbling brick structures along the Merrimack River looked like carcasses of dinosaurs," said Kamen. "I could also see that the buildings were prime real estate—waterfront property right in the middle of the city and going for a song."

Since 1982 Dean has renovated several of the factories and warehouses and put them back into circulation as office space and light-industry workshops. "Now this area has really caught on; more than a hundred companies have moved into the renovated buildings, and property values have gone berserk—sky high."

Some of the credit for Kamen's successful venture goes to Manchester's phenomenal growth in the last ten years. Rated by *U.S. News and World Report* in 1986 as one of the cities where business is best, Manchester has been attracting an impressive roster of high-tech companies. New Hampshire's favorable tax rates (much lower than in Massachusetts), the city's easy access to Boston, and what Dean calls "a lovely vacation environment" less than an hour from beaches and mountains, have created a winning combination.

Boom times have also come to Portland, Maine, one of the cities that suffered most from economic stagnation between World War I and the 1960s. Today Portland has turned its economy around, finding prosperity as the banking and commercial center of the state. On streets cobbled with ballast stones, vintage buildings preserve the 19th-century flavor of the town and enjoy new life as shops, art galleries, and busy restaurants.

Bounded on three sides by the bountiful waters of Casco Bay, the city charms a visitor with vistas of an island-dotted sea: sunlight flaring on white sails, waves cresting with foam in wind that carries the tang of salt, fishing boats and port traffic of ferries and tugs emerging from tattered curtains of fog. These scenic shores have been immortalized in the paintings of local 19th-century artist Winslow Homer and have inspired Andrew Wyeth, Fitz Hugh Lane, Marsden Hartley, and countless other painters who, over the years, have found their muses in Maine.

"We artists may be as big as Maine's potato industry, with respect to the income we earn and generate. Right now, there must be 200 of us here," said Sherry Miller, dabbing intense fuchsia on a canvas in her studio, which was filled with vivid images of the tropics. The active art scene has spawned an assortment of galleries to showcase this profusion of Maine talent.

Some restaurants hold exhibitions so customers can savor metaphors of form and color with their omelets. As for the masterpieces, they have taken up residence in the opulent new wing of the Portland Art Museum and in the small but elegant Joan Whitney Payson Gallery.

The small-town sense of community in Portland drew city councilor and former mayor Pamela P. Plumb and her lawyer husband, Peter, "from away," and the growing cultural attractions, which they helped nourish, have kept them there. "Another consideration was the easy access to sailing. Now we live five minutes from the water," said Pam, a trim, soft-spoken political activist. "On a nice summer evening we'll grab a bunch of mussels off the rocks as part of supper on our sailboat. We also have a Boston whaler, which is our car in summer; we rent a house on one of the islands offshore."

Life-style also lures people to Burlington, Vermont, a city of just under 40,000 with a sizable number of transplants. In 1988 the U.S. Conference of Mayors voted Burlington and Frederick, Maryland, the two most livable cities in the country with populations below 100,000. The judges singled out Burlington's wealth of cultural offerings, but no one can overlook its lovely location on the shores of Lake Champlain and its mountain views. To live in Burlington is to feel at firsthand the exhilaration of the outdoors, to see the lake shimmer with gold as the sun sinks behind the Adirondacks, and to sail, fish, ski, hike, or stretch out on the grass to hear a twilight concert.

Bernard Sanders, the town's outspoken socialist mayor, is an expatriate from Brooklyn, New York. He had much to say

about what makes Burlington special. I met him in city hall, a stately white building with a gold cupola. "Burlington is a place where the individual still matters and grocers still give credit, where business people walk to their appointments, where tall buildings are not allowed. People here have a healthy respect for the environment. There's a vitality and an activism that makes this an exciting city," said Sanders, a vigorous man of middle age. Then he paused for a moment and added, "But a good delicatessen wouldn't hurt."

"People are really what make Burlington different," he continued. "The population is an interesting mix of native Vermonters from a hardworking farming tradition and professionals from the big cities, particularly New York, who are prepared to sacrifice income to live here. They are the kind of people who feel there's something more important in life than making money." Proving the point is singing teacher William Reed. He works 35 hours in three days in New York City training operatic voices for the stage so he can spend the rest of the week with his family in Vermont, leading what he calls a Currier and Ives existence.

From Burlington it is a lovely drive through the forested Green Mountains to Montpelier, Vermont, the smallest state capital in the country. A diminutive city of 9,000, it is wedged in so narrow a valley

that the gold dome of its statehouse sparkles like a jewel embedded in a setting of hills. Inside the building some years ago legislators passed Act 250 in a determined effort to control development. As a result, plans to build a large shopping mall outside of Burlington in 1978 were defeated, allaying, at least for a while, a threat to the city's small-town charm.

Malls are, however, as much a feature of the New England landscape as in other regions, and Providence, Rhode Island, lays claim to the granddaddy of them all—an indoor arcade built in 1828. But perhaps the best known presence in Providence is Brown University. I strolled from where it sits on College Hill down to the brick sidewalks of mile-long Benefit Street, a showcase of architecture: Italian Renaissance mansions, steepled colonial churches, a Greek Revival Athenaeum, and Federal-style homes of 18th-century sea captains and merchants. In all there are 200 restored buildings, including several that belong to the Rhode Island School of Design (or RISD, pronounced rizdee).

Praised as the Harvard of art institutions, RISD hums with activity. Many of the classrooms are studios, and going from one department to another I heard the ring of a hammer on metal in a jewelry class, the whine of saws in the furniture shop, the thud of looms, the roar of glassblowing furnaces and ceramic kilns. I saw students painting, sculpting, setting type, and designing landscapes, dresses, and packaging. Dominating all the bustle was the silent intensity of young artists and craftsmen striving to create beauty.

RISD was established in 1877 to train artisans for the textile and costume-jewelry industries. As happened in so much of New England, beginning in the 1920s, most of

*On Boston's stylish Newbury Street, a
thoroughfare of restaurants, galleries,
and boutiques, a clerk at a vintage-
clothing store displays her collection.*

Providence's cotton mills moved to the South, but the city still manufactures more costume jewelry than any other place in the country. Along with tourism, it is a top income earner in the state.

"There are about 850 firms, from one-man shops to plants like ours," said James Winoker, leading me to the factory floor of his company, B. B. Greenberg. The firm molds plastics, casts metal, and stamps brass for jewelry at prices almost anyone can afford. Women sat at long tables, some meticulously applying epoxy color to metal brooches with hypodermic needles, others rapidly inspecting lipstick cases for imperfections. Earrings, each with a tiny rubber sleeve over its steel post (so it would not be electroplated) were awaiting a gold bath. Hundreds of chains, hanging on racks, were immersed in the acrid liquid, slowly acquiring the sheen shoppers want.

Those same shoppers, if they wish, can dine royally in Providence. George Germon and Johanne Killeen, who have been rated among the best new chefs in the country, attract clientele from all over New England for their baked pastas, their herb-roasted chicken, and their thin, crisp pizzas, grilled over a wood fire. "We season in a simple way, without smothering our meats in sauces or using too many spices," said George in one of their restaurants, Al Forno, which was redolent of olive oil and garlic. "Our food has to look good as well as taste good, for we consider ourselves artists, tempting the eye as well as the palate of our patrons."

The culinary arts in Providence have received another big boost from Johnson and Wales University, a cooking school that enrolls 2,400 students. In a classroom lined with ovens and scented with the warm, yeasty aroma of baking bread, dean and master chef Robert M. Nograd talked with me about the changing eating habits of Americans. "This country was created by hungry people. Dining was a matter of quantity until the 1960s, when Americans started to discover fine foods," said Nograd, in softly accented English revealing his Hungarian ancestry.

In another kitchen—there are 26 of them at the school—I watched students, all in white uniforms and tall hats, carve celery, carrots, and radishes into flowers. Next door freshmen were learning the technique of cooking in woks. One serving of egg foo yong was a flop. The oil wasn't hot enough, the chef explained to the class huddled around the stove.

While good food graces Providence tables, good theater enlivens its stages, most notably at the award-winning Trinity Repertory Company. It began in 1964 as a small, financially troubled troupe presenting plays in a church and has evolved into a highly respected professional organization noted for its imaginative productions, which draw some 20,000 subscribers.

Theater in Connecticut has also defined a special place for itself, and it by no means languishes in the shadow of New York's Great White Way. For many years such places as the Shubert Theater in New Haven were merely tryout houses for plays before they opened on Broadway. Now the acclaimed Long Wharf and Yale Repertory Theaters in New Haven select plays, cast the actors, and create the staging for some of the most innovative, important works in American theater. A dozen plays that were first brought to life at the Yale Rep have gone on to international fame. Eleven productions, including the hits *Annie, Shenandoah,* and *Man of La*

Mancha, premiered at the Goodspeed Opera House, a Victorian showplace on the banks of the Connecticut River in rural East Haddam, the only theater in the country dedicated to the American musical.

While Broadway may still mean the big time, it no longer dominates serious theater. "You can see 25 first-class plays a year and never set foot out of Connecticut," said Benjamin Mordecai, Managing Director of the Yale School of Drama and the Yale Rep. "For a state with a population of a mere three million to have that much theater is extraordinary." The magic comes from the drama school, hailed for its great influence on contemporary theater. Its graduates have remarkable track records, and they populate the entire realm of the professional stage. Its former students include actresses Meryl Streep and Sigourney Weaver and director Elia Kazan.

Alumnus George C. White also plays a stellar role, and his accomplishments and awards fill a printed page. I met him when he was wearing the hat of Founder and President of the Eugene O'Neill Theater Center on the shores of Long Island Sound in Waterford, Connecticut. "One of our programs is a 14-week boot camp in basics for college students who want to go into the theater. It gives kids a real dose of reality, so they understand what such a career involves. We're interested in survivors, not graduates," said George, as we watched a student group run through a dance sequence for the fourth time.

For more than 20 years the center has staged readings of new works for audiences that come from all over the country to preview budding talent. "From some 1,500 entries each year we select 12 or 15 scripts. *Agnes of God* made its debut here, as did the award-winning *Fences*. A play isn't finished until you put it on its feet in front of an audience. If people start feeling their chairs, you know you've lost them."

In my travels through New England every stop rewarded me with the beauty or the power of human endeavor.

In the kaleidoscope of my memories the summer landscape of the Berkshires shimmers with a marvelous mosaic of music, theater, dance, and art: Shakespeare performed on the lawn of novelist Edith Wharton's estate; the dramatic choreography of dancers and strobe lights at the Jacob's Pillow Festival, a fountainhead of modern dance; sunlight creating shadows on modern sculpture in the gardens of Chesterwood; the curtain rising at the Williamstown Theater Festival; Baroque music played on original instruments at the Aston Magna Festival; Leonard Bernstein bringing his passion for music to thousands at the Tanglewood Music Festival; radiant Renoir paintings—34 of them—and other prize Impressionist works at the Sterling and Francine Clark Art Institute in Williamstown.

Robert Sterling Clark, whose private collection created this small gem of a museum, once wrote in his diary, "Outside of necessities of life . . . art in all its manifestations, plastic, literary, musical, legal, medical, military, equestrian, and culinary was the greatest thing in life." Poverty, crime, and drug problems plague the places I visited, but my quest was for the great things in life. And in New England I found them —and never felt the chairs.

ES WHARF FERRY TERMINAL

Commuting by ferry eases rush hour for Boston-bound workers. Five boats make some twenty trips a day from the South Shore to Rowes Wharf on the downtown waterfront, where a businessman (above) takes in the bustle of the harbor. A water shuttle also links the city and Logan International Airport. Boston proper, with 600,000 inhabitants, stands at the heart of a metropolitan area of a hundred cities and towns with a population totaling three million.

On the waterfront, a ferry leaves Rowes Wharf. The brick archway connects a hotel, an office tower,

and a complex of luxury condominiums. The domed pavilion provides a waiting room for passengers.

Sunlight streams through the great windows in the fifth-floor reading room of the Boston Athenaeum, one of the oldest private libraries in the country. Established in 1807, the institution owns more than 700,000 volumes, including most of George Washington's library. Gas street lamps (left) enhance the charm of Acorn Street on Beacon Hill. Domain of Boston Brahmins in the 19th century, this neighborhood now draws affluent young professionals. The North End (below)—first Irish, then Jewish, now Italian—faces a new wave of immigrants: more yuppies, who are renovating tenements and converting wharfside warehouses to apartments.

Four-mile run brings a blur of racers to Commonwealth Avenue. A city of sports fans, Boston sponsors

a famous marathon and supports wildly popular baseball, basketball, football, and hockey teams.

Halls of academe: Across the Charles River from Boston sprawls Harvard University, the country's oldest institution of higher learning, founded in 1636. Sharing a Cambridge location, the Massachusetts Institute of Technology has become a bastion of science and engineering. The Maclaurin building (lower right) houses labs and lecture halls. In New Haven, Connecticut, a Gothic window in the Harkness Tower (right) looks out onto Yale University.

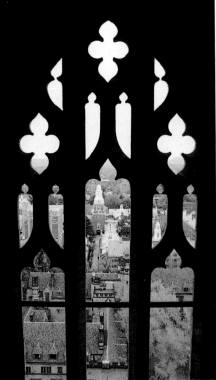

On stage in the Goodspeed Opera House in East Haddam, Connecticut, actors cavort in the 1920s musical Mr. Cinders, *a comic version of the Cinderella story. In sumptuous gilt-and-velvet Victorian style, the 398-seat theater, devoted entirely to musicals, has seen nearly a hundred revivals since 1963 and has launched ten new shows. Getting an early start in show business, Matthew Lee, age 11 (below, at right), and Wolfe Coleman, 4, play in costume and with props at Shakespeare & Company in Lenox, Massachusetts. One of five major summer theaters in the Berkshires, it also brings Shakespeare to some 50,000 young students each year.*

Defying gravity with athletic grace, a
dancer (below) with the David Parsons
Company performs at the Jacob's
Pillow Dance Festival in the
Berkshires. "The Pillow supports
young artists and provides a perfect
creative atmosphere in a beautiful
hillside setting," says choreographer
David Parsons, dancing at left with
Denise Roberts. Founded in 1933 by
Ted Shawn, a pioneer in modern
dance, the center also offers workshops
for the artists of tomorrow.

Glittering four-day gala at Tanglewood celebrates the 70th birthday of composer, conductor, and pianist Leonard Bernstein. Under a tent on the Tanglewood grounds, the maestro chats with Broadway personality Kitty Carlisle at a dinner for 600 (below left). A picnic table set with special flair reserves a place on the lawn (below right), where thousands gathered to hear tributes and selections from Bernstein's music. Thousands more sat inside the Music Shed. Proceeds from the extravaganza, whose tickets cost up to $5,000 each, augmented the scholarship fund for Tanglewood's summer teaching program, where Bernstein himself studied in 1940. Dressed in regulation white, members of the Boston Symphony Orchestra (right) run through their parts before the final concert, led by Bernstein.

"The intensity of the light brings painters to Cape Cod," says Paul Resika (below). "And the long luminous twilights are full of feeling and sentiment." Here in his summer studio in Truro, Massachusetts, Resika stands beside his painting of a pier in adjacent Provincetown. In a garden setting, Henry Henches (left) paints a portrait of a student as part of a demonstration at the Provincetown Art School. Some 50 galleries on the cape exhibit the works of established and emerging artists. A mecca for the avant-garde since the turn of the century, the outer cape also attracts more traditional writers and scholars. Eugene O'Neill wrote many of his plays here, and the production of Bound East for Cardiff *by the Provincetown Players in 1916 launched his career.*

Lunching alfresco, guests gather on an estate in Stockbridge, Massachusetts. Once a summer resort for

New York and Boston society, the Berkshires have become a favored haunt of artists and intellectuals.

Marble dome of the Rhode Island State House dominates downtown Providence. Beyond the business district lies Narragansett Bay, which connects the city to the ocean 27 miles away. Though Providence once thrived on trade and industry, it later fell on hard times; recently, high-tech firms have helped turn the economic tide, and redevelopment is giving the city a new look. The past lives on along historic Benefit Street (below), lined with the restored homes of sea captains, silversmiths, and merchants. Gaslights and brick sidewalks add to the atmosphere.

Mallets aloft, polo players charge at full gallop in a match between North American and Argentinian all-stars at the Greenwich Polo Club in Connecticut. Here an Argentinian in blue and white whacks the ball toward the goal. Spectators (right) coolly appraise the action; a graceful still life (left) marks someone's spot.

V

THE ROADS LESS TRAVELED

By Jane R. McCauley   Photographs by Michael Melford

"Nature is my only boss," said Carver Crowell, cranberry farmer. "I can walk out of my house and look across my fields and say, this is all mine. And the only thing I have to worry about is nature."

Carver cultivates 70 acres of cranberries in Harwich Port, Massachusetts, about halfway along the fishhook curve of the Cape Cod peninsula. For most of his life he has been tied to the land, and his affection for it is convincing—for cultivating cranberries is hard work.

Carver stays up nights to turn on the sprinklers if there's a frost. He slips and slides through ditches full of icy water and hopes the sun will come out. He puts in backbreaking hours pruning vines; he races against the clock to save a crop when a water main breaks. And harvest brings

grueling 14-hour days, seven days a week, rain or shine.

"But I love the land," he told me. "And I think love of land is why farmers are farmers." That devotion to the land, that proud independence, that sunup-to-sundown work ethic are not unique to Carver. All along New England's byways—from Connecticut to Maine—I found those attributes running deep. I spent days rambling through quiet villages crowned with white steeples, and on other days I followed twisting roads to picturesque farmhouses. I shared in community rituals—county fairs, hymn

Small-town symbol, the steeple of the Congregational Church in Peacham, Vermont, gets a fresh coat of classic white paint. More New England symbols, scarecrows (above) appear along rural roadsides.

sings, Friday high school football games, baked-bean suppers.

I visited places where doors are never locked, where roadside vegetable stands are run on the honor system, and towns where the bonds of church and family are still strong. By journey's end, I too had felt the pull of splendid scenery, neighborliness, and a simpler life. I understood why people who leave this countryside often come back.

Tall, soft-spoken, tanned by sun and wind, Carver Crowell is one of them. He returned to Cape Cod one summer ten years ago just to help his father—and wound up staying.

When I caught up with him he was facing that autumn's harvest. The summer visitors had left Harwich Port, and many of the waterfront cottages and stores had closed. A graceful, unhurried pace had settled once more upon the town.

It was already hot at 7:30 in the morning when Carver and I walked around his property. It hardly resembled a farm: There were no barns or animals, only acres of flat bottomland mazed by dusty paths.

During harvest, Carver told me, the bogs are flooded, and a tractor-like piece of machinery lumbers through them, knocking berries off the vines. They float there, creating spectacular seas of deep crimson. With long rakes, harvesters corral the cranberries into chutes that lead to trucks, which haul the berries away.

Each season a thin layer of sand is spread in the bogs, a practice begun in 1816 when a local man named Henry Hall noticed that the wild vines growing near the ocean-side sand dunes produced more berries than vines growing farther inland.

Ninety percent of the berries are harvested wet, Carver told me, but they're only suitable for juice or canning. The berries we buy in bags in supermarkets are picked dry, usually with mechanical harvesters. They bring a premium on the fresh-fruit market, and the market for cranberries is a good one. Massachusetts, the leading producer, has more than 12,000 acres of bogs blanketing Bristol, Plymouth, Nantucket, and Barnstable Counties.

Out on the bogs, Carver cautioned me to step gingerly, for at the slightest nudge berries would drop. Thousands dangled from the web of green vines, like miniature Christmas-tree balls. Sprinklers crisscrossed the bog.

"Frost kills the buds in the spring and softens the berries in the fall," Carver told me. "Then they gum up the machinery at the processing plant." So the sprinklers help protect the berries from frost.

"As the water freezes around them, it insulates them from the cold." Carver vividly remembers one heartbreaking night before he had sprinklers when he lost about half his crop. Now a cable from an outdoor thermometer runs to another in his bedroom, so when the temperature begins to drop he's the first one into the bogs, scraping ice from the sprinklers all night if necessary to keep them flowing.

Carver admits that sometimes the thought of selling his land has some appeal. "Nature can beat the pants off of you," he said. But I sensed that the bonds are too strong for him to give up. "With hard work and a little luck," he says. . . .

Hard work and a little luck are themes, too, in the northwest corner of Connecticut, where geography and a determined citizenry have combined to preserve a yesteryear flavor. No major highways or cities interrupt the pastoral feel of the area. The roller-coaster foothills of the Berkshires run through thick forests, through meadows tawny in autumn, and through fields ringed by aging stone walls. Coursing south from Massachusetts, the waters of the Housatonic River brim with trout, and on its shadowed banks the Appalachian Trail wends north and south, toward Maine or Georgia.

This is a landscape of many moods. In sunlight the river gurgles and the leaves toss and turn, frolicking in the breezes. When fog and mist cloak the hills and valleys, the land seems to brood and pout. Nights are often hauntingly silent, as they can be in the country, and sounds seem to whisper through the treetops. In the darkness the moon looms bright. It became a beacon of comfort for this often-lost traveler, for road signs are few and far between.

"It's like a separate state," one resident said. To wander through the sleepy towns of Kent, Sharon, and Cornwall, which overlook the Housatonic, evokes memories of eras gone by. It's like flipping through the pages of a Grandma Moses album. Not much traffic courses the towns' main streets, which are lined with prim, clapboard houses and quaint shops.

Some of the shops display the works of the area's artists and artisans, many of whom were attracted here by the idyllic setting. They have converted barns into studios, been inspired by the beauty around them, and found the solitude and quiet that help them create.

Todd Piker, a potter, lives in the village of Cornwall Bridge with his wife, Ivelisse,

herself a talented leather worker, and their two daughters. For his glazes he utilizes materials from the local soil, including a mineral by-product created by an iron-smelting industry in the late 18th and early 19th centuries.

Todd and his assistants produce some 30 tons of hand-thrown pottery a year. He describes his pieces as "folk works," pottery that is functional rather than whimsical.

He established his studio here in 1972 when he was 19, converting a shed on the property into a 35-foot-long brick-and-clay kiln that resembles a long igloo. "The area's beauty and the people have both embraced me," he says, having achieved a gratifying fame.

Inside the domed kiln, stair-step levels can hold a thousand pieces. Outside, cords of wood abut the kiln, for it is wood firing, in part, that makes Todd's work unique. As the flame intensifies inside the kiln, he told me, it licks higher and higher, touching and randomly patterning each object, so no two pieces are the same.

I asked him why he works with clay. "I'm not an exacting person," he said. "So I like the margin for error that clay's plasticity permits me." His ease with the medium was evident as I watched him throw a pot. "You can't pull clay apart," he said, over the steady hum of his wheel. "It must be *coaxed* apart." The shapeless mound rapidly became a pitcher. His motions were smooth and methodical. "Clay is magical stuff," he said. Indeed, in his hands it was.

And in the hands of Stephen Fellerman, whose studio is nearby, molten glass is equally magical. Stephen is recognized as one of the country's foremost glassblowers. His studio and an upstairs gallery occupy a rustic barn alongside the Housatonic in Kent.

When I arrived, Stephen and an assistant were getting ready for a craft fair. Sweat poured down Stephen's face as he rotated a long tube with a molten glob of glass at the end that was in the furnace. "I've always been fascinated with fire and heat," he told me. He is largely self-taught and only recently has taken time out to attend classes, searching for a new direction for his work. When he first came to Kent in the '70s he had no gallery and no stores in which to market his wares. He supported himself by making art nouveau-style glass, which was much in demand by glass collectors.

He described his approach to me as "a painterly one," a process of adding swirls of color to his work and encasing it in black or clear glass. His lamps, vases, perfume bottles, and sculptures were pleasing blends, I thought, of traditional and contemporary elements.

Of all the fine crafts I saw during my tour through New England, none seemed more appropriate than cabinetmaker Ian Ingersoll's Shaker-style furniture. His chairs, cabinets, and tables embody the pure, functional lines favored by the Shakers. Descended from generations of New Englanders, Ian believes his heritage is linked to that of the Shakers; their religious communities once were thick in this part of New England.

"I try to do cabinetmaking as it might have been done 200 years ago," he told me, "utilizing old designs and styles. There are no tricks or secrets to woodworking, though I *do* have an eye that I've developed during 15 years of making Shaker furniture. So naturally I see things that others might not. What still touches a deep chord in me is the asymmetry that is typical of this furniture."

Ian's shop is housed in the former tollhouse at the foot of an old red covered bridge linking Sharon with West Cornwall, one of the several little communities that make up Cornwall. Main Street winds uphill past Ian's shop, past Cadwell's coffee shop, past a bookstore, a restaurant, the post office, a market, and Todd Piker's retail shop. Built around 1864, the bridge is one of only two in the state that still carry automobiles. It is a landmark the town is proud of. And though the state owns the bridge, the residents of West Cornwall regard it as their own. In the 1940s, square dances were held in it, and legend has it that one fellow with a teetotaler wife stored his whiskey among its timbers.

On the bright morning I drove across, the boards clanked and rattled. Upstream a fisherman in waders was casting for trout. A painter with brush and bucket was covering the bright red of the bridge with a muted brick-red tone.

At the local antiquarian bookshop the sign read, "Hours by chance or appointment." By chance, owner Barbara Farnsworth was in, and she talked with me about the bridge and the feuding that had been going on between the town and the state. "Last summer the state painted the bridge that awful red," she said in a crisp New England accent. "It was closed from 9 a.m. to 4 p.m. every day for five weeks, so we had to drive miles out of our way. Outsiders, who didn't know the back roads, were lost."

The town also lost some revenue when tourists couldn't reach local campgrounds, and townspeople were somewhat annoyed, too, that the paint job wasn't offered to a local contractor.

Harry L. Colley, a village resident, spearheaded an appeal to the state to repaint the

bridge. "Most people here were appalled at the new color," he told me. "Even tourists commented on it."

"Traditionally, covered bridges were tinted brick-red with a stain that would weather and fade," Harry said. "But the state used an oil-base paint that won't weather. They didn't realize that when the leaves were off the trees that bridge would have stuck out like a sore thumb."

The involvement of the citizens in the bridge controversy interested me. True, New Englanders take a deep pride in their rich past, and the exercise of the democratic process is a tradition deeply fixed in the region. Here, after all, town meetings have long given citizens the opportunity to champion causes, speak their pieces, and influence public policy.

Town meetings evolved from early gatherings in New England, and though they have been attempted in other parts of the country, the idea has not really caught on elsewhere. They may be the most often praised examples of direct democracy.

Held usually once a year in the spring, they settle questions of taxation, zoning and planning, and new programs. An agenda—or "warrant"—is posted before the meeting, listing items to be taken up. Any voter can speak on any subject that appears on the agenda.

Town meetings were once an eagerly anticipated social event that lasted all day and included a hearty noon meal prepared by the women. Today, however, complex issues and a larger population have made necessary a few changes in the form of some town meetings, but local passions are keeping the institution alive.

Agricultural fairs are a newer phenomenon than town meetings, but similar passions are keeping them alive, too, in spite of the decline of farming in New England in recent years. Among the oldest of the agricultural societies in the U.S.—the organizations that sponsor the fairs—are those of Maine. And each autumn, as it has for 138 years, the West Oxford Agricultural Society plays host to the Fryeburg Fair in Fryeburg. The eight-day event is the state's largest fair; in 1988 it drew a record crowd of more than 123,000 people.

When I arrived at about 10 a.m. on opening day, the fairgrounds were already bustling. Near the entrance, in the middle of a grassy square, a blind accordionist performed as people on benches nearby applauded and tapped their feet. I wandered on, through long halls filled with baked goods, photographic exhibitions, artwork, quilts, and dried flower arrangements. There were tractor-pulling contests, frying-pan tosses, and sheepherding competitions. Inside barns enormous cattle lowed and chewed; outside, an ornery bull kicked as it was being hosed down.

Young 4-H'ers—both boys and girls— pitched hay in stalls, with hard-won ribbons blossoming on beams overhead. In the sheep barn I scratched a few woolly backs, then watched a shearing demonstration. In the rabbit barn I *oohed* and *aahed* at floppy ears and twitching noses.

The sound of country music lured me to

a small platform where cloggers were dancing. The group—ten young girls—was known as the Maine Attraction. In white frilly dresses and white shoes and socks they stomped and thumped and twirled. They were from tiny Arundel in southwestern Maine, a town with no high school and no post office.

"We have competed locally and in the South," said Tasha Walker, during a break in the dancing. At 15 she was the youngest clogging leader in New England. "And we placed second in the national finals." The crowd applauded and gave donations.

I passed most of my time at the fair wandering the midway. Music blared; and multihued lights flashed like psychedelic rainbows from revolving rides. Bags of pink and green cotton candy dangled in vendors' stands; in my memory cotton candy was always eaten in wads from a stick. Hot dogs, burgers, and oversize onion rings sizzled on grills, and the pungent odor of steaming clams wafted through the midway crowd.

"Come on, try your hand!" barkers yelled. "Only two bucks." I threw a few darts, tossed a few rings, spent more than two bucks, and won a stuffed California-Raisin figure and a mug. Enough excitement, I decided, for one day.

Few New England agricultural fairs are as large or as modern as Fryeburg's, but nearly every town has some kind of fall celebration—a time for letting go before the onset of winter.

So autumn is a festive season, with firehouse auctions, yard sales, and church suppers and bazaars. Other festivals celebrate the annual foliage extravaganza when tourists—"leaf peepers"—arrive in droves, jamming inns and motels and cruising roadways. The eruption of color

along the back roads is unrivaled as a spectacle, but the automobile, I believe, is not necessarily the best vehicle for seeing it. So in Vermont I traded my car for a bicycle.

Vermont's array of hardwoods produces a particularly splashy show. The state is sparsely settled, with the second-lowest population density in New England. Gentle hills and valleys cradle farmlands and small restful towns. Legislative mandates have left the roadsides free of billboards, and strict land-use laws have helped keep much of the state unspoiled.

Many Vermonters enjoy a wholesome life-style, pursuing the many and diverse opportunities for outdoor recreation that their state offers. Numerous cycling outfitters have evolved in the state since John Freidin established Vermont Bicycle Touring (VBT) in 1972. It was the first to offer inn-to-inn bicycling vacations, and one weekend I joined 19 other riders for a ramble through the countryside around the towns of Bridgewater and Woodstock.

Our weekend began on a rainy Friday afternoon at the October Country Inn just off U.S. Route 4 in Bridgewater Corners. Witty and bearded Richard Sims shares ownership of the large farmhouse with Patrick Runkel. Homespun furnishings spread throughout the nine rooms encourage a casual atmosphere. A book-lined library leads into the living room, which has a stone fireplace and a century-old wood-burning stove.

Meals, prepared chiefly by Patrick, were a big hit with everyone. We enjoyed French and Greek cuisine, as well as hearty American breakfasts. Friday's dinner consisted of a spicy ginger-carrot soup, fresh sole baked in wine, zucchini, and sourdough bread.

We were a mixed group of mostly "flat-landers"—people born out of state—who gathered after dinner in the living room. Bob and Ann Dunlap had come with Madeleine and Norman Gaut to celebrate Norman's birthday. Canadian Suzanne Lewis was satisfying an ambition she had had for 17 years. Two friends, Catherine Fauquier and Nancy Lockhart, had joined her. After the introductions, VBT leaders Mary Miller and Jerome Milks gave us helpful advice for the two-day excursion, and a preview. "There's some good foliage out there, especially on the upper slopes," said Mary. "That should be incentive for you to hit the high spots." Later I stepped outside into the brilliant night and whiffed the cold air, ripe with the promise of frost and clear skies for the weekend.

Our wake-up call came at 7 a.m. and was followed by a briefing by Jerome on the handling of our 12-speed bikes. Then, after breakfast and an animated discussion of the days' routes, we were off. Our course took us along Route 4, heavily trafficked on this morning, into Woodstock.

"So far, so good," I thought to myself as I pedaled the first eight miles into town. I savored the sunshine on my face, the crisp weather, and the leaves pirouetting in their final dances. People waved from their houses, and an occasional dog yapped. The tall flag on the back of my bike flapped back and forth in time with my pedaling.

With the others I swept past the oval village green, where the Chamber of Commerce booth stood. After crossing the Middle Covered Bridge, we turned onto River Street. Woodstock's elegant homes and affluent aura quietly subsided into grassy fields backed by steep slopes.

I fell behind the others for a while and soon found myself winding uphill on a gravel path through birches, maples, and oaks. I struggled to make the ascent. I remembered Mary's advice from the night before: "Vermont is hilly." (I think she meant mountainous.) "Go into the hills easy at first. Climb them with dignity. Relax your shoulders. Take breaks." My thighs began to ache, and sweat dripped from beneath my yellow helmet. Though a regular at aerobic exercising, I felt miserably out of shape.

So I heaved a sigh of relief when I reached flatter ground in Barnard and parked my bike beside the shimmering waters of Silver Lake, a favorite swimming hole for bikers. But on this brisk day I opted for a roast beef sandwich and a Coke instead of a swim. Mary, who had arrived before me, had already finished her lunch. Her biking career began after college, she told me, when she had toured Europe with a friend. She has been leading VBT tours since 1980 and recently completed one in New Zealand.

The afternoon included a visit to Quechee Gorge, a deep and beautiful ravine cut by the Ottauquechee River and rimmed by fragrant pines.

By day's end I was sure I had gone more than 40 miles, and I had the aches and pains to prove it. Other riders, to my amazement, had chosen alternate routes for the day and biked as much as 77 miles. But such strenuous activity didn't affect the conviviality back at the October Country Inn that night. Some talked quietly before a blazing fire while others played board games in the dining room. By 11:30, though, the only sounds in the inn were the crackling of the dying embers and the steady purring of a cat.

The fine weather held for Sunday, and I awakened refreshed and eager to go. Fluffy clouds drifted in the sky as we rode south along Vermont's scenic Route 100. Scarecrows, pumpkins, and tidy woodpiles brightened roadsides and front porches. Shadows curled around hillsides that were crossed by swaths of russets and golds.

Our biggest challenge came on "hysteria hill," appropriately named by a former VBT group for its nearly vertical incline. We huffed and puffed, and most of us ended up walking our bikes to the top. We tarried in the restored village of Plymouth, birthplace of Calvin Coolidge, wandering into its cheese factory, store, museum, and barns. From there the ride was pure ecstasy, a long downhill coast.

Our bike trip ended that afternoon, but as I continued my travels through New England I would often think back on my biking companions and the sights and sounds we shared: the faint murmur of a train, the swish of a cow's tail, the call of a crow high in a tree. Biking through Vermont had brought me closer to the countryside and deepened my affection for it.

But now it was on to Vermont's Northeast Kingdom for a Sunday evening hymn sing. In the 1940s Senator George Aiken, moved by the region's beauty, coined the phrase "Northeast Kingdom" for his state's isolated northeastern corner, a realm of red barns attached to houses, of log lodges, and of snug lakeside cottages. "Vermont distilled to its essence," Fodor's 1989 New England guidebook describes it.

Slopes here tumble into amber pasturelands, into myriad lakes, and into dense forests that stretch north to Canada. A tangle of narrow roads, a particularly charming feature, has apparently neither end nor beginning. Rambling drives make possible

a pleasant stumble onto the unexpected.

Certainly that's how it was when I found the Old North Church. "You will think you're in the middle of nowhere," a woman in North Danville had said when I asked directions. I drove and drove along unpaved roads through fields and woods and the desolation of a black night, not knowing whether I was going north, east, south, or west. Finally a white church awash in moonlight welcomed me. Lanterns flickered a warm greeting from the arched windows, and the red doors creaked when I opened them and went in. The Reverend Scudder Parker was speaking on the closer relationship these days between urban and rural lives — "Country and City: Saving Each Other."

Built in 1832 and owned today by the Danville Historical Society, the church lacks heat and electricity (parts of the Northeast Kingdom did not get electricity until the 1960s), so it closes during the cold months. But since 1957 half a dozen or so of these lamplight services have been held each summer.

About 100 worshipers sat in the straight-backed pews, many holding flashlights or candles. Some wore jeans. A fretful young child wailed.

After the sermon, people called out their favorite hymns as organist Shirley Langmaid pumped an old pipe organ. We sang verses from "Amazing Grace," from "We've a Story to Tell to the Nations," and from hymn number 132, "I Will Remember Thee." Outside, the pines shuddered in the wind, and twinkling stars shone in the sky like glitter on black velvet.

The service was touching, one of the most memorable occasions of my travels through New England. I understood why the Old North Church draws visitors not

Still common in rural areas, weather vanes point to the source of a wind. A copper vane of a Morgan horse tops a barn near Colebrook, New Hampshire.

only from across the state, but also from across the country.

I dropped in on a variety of church services during my travels through New England. Nearly all were well attended, for in the little towns the church is not only a center of worship but often is also a social center. Church suppers are especially popular, and in Vermont I saw a number of handwritten notices of chicken potpie dinners.

In parts of Maine baked beans on Saturday night have been the custom since the 1940s. So one Saturday night I stopped by the First Congregational Church in Pittston, where the second of three seatings for a bean supper was well under way in the fellowship hall. Despite a heavy downpour, guests had begun patiently lining up outside an hour and a half before the 5 o'clock dinner.

In the kitchen, pots of dark brown beans had been simmering for hours, and casseroles, plates of strawberry shortcake with globs of whipped cream, and platters of steamed brown bread covered the counters. One woman took a moment to reminisce about the days when the food was cooked on wood-burning stoves, and the milk was brought in in metal cans. Bob Bragdon, one of the hosts, ran through the list of ingredients used to cook the beans: molasses, mustard, salt, brown sugar, salt pork. In some places in New England, he said, the beans are cooked in the ground for about 24 hours.

Hearty eaters lined long tables, and the hum of conversation rose amid the clatter of silverware. "Many people think we offer the best meal in the area," Bob's wife, Ruth, said. "And we'll serve 150 tonight."

What with the warmth of my welcome, I was soon caught up in the festivity of the evening. New Englanders have been ac-

cused of being taciturn, even aloof, but I found them generous and friendly, eager to share meals and to chat. Church functions, I learned, were invariably an excellent introduction to the people of a locality; and so were the local stores.

Competition from the large chain stores has not yet eliminated from the New England countryside the old-fashioned neighborhood store, and poking through one is a pleasant way to pass a few hours.

Among the oldest that I dropped in on was the Tinkerville Country Store, which has been in operation for more than a hundred years in western New Hampshire. "Two roads diverged in a wood, and I— I took the one less traveled by . . . ," wrote poet Robert Frost, longtime resident of New Hampshire. I did the same, turning off U.S. Highway 302 onto New Hampshire 112 toward the hamlet of Tinkerville, whose improbable name acted as a lure.

"Welcome to the Tinkerville Mall," joked a patron when I found the wooden, glass-front store. Its interior was a hodgepodge: bottles, cans, T-shirts, dog biscuits, sunglasses, jars of dill pickles. A glass case just inside the door held various candies: Tootsie Rolls, lollipops, licorice strings. Housewares and groceries cluttered every shelf and cabinet. "Years ago," said Lorraine Bezanson, who was behind the counter, "the store sold a line of hunting clothes. And also organs."

"Pipe organs?"

"Yup."

Lorraine and her husband, Paul, run the store. "We loved Tinkerville," she told me, "so we moved here from Amesbury, Massachusetts, after spending several summers camping in the area." Blond and quiet Stacy Aldrich was busy helping out, as he does on weekends.

Once a booming mining town with a few thousand people, Tinkerville has seen its population shrink until little remains except a few houses, farms, and White Mountain Stitching, a factory employing about 25 people.

Lorraine and Paul live beside the store. "That's the only way we can manage it," Lorraine said. "We're open every day from 6:30 a.m. to 9 p.m., except for a few hours on Christmas."

The New England general store has long been the source of common—and not-so-common—day-to-day needs of citizens. An account published by the Little Compton Historical Society of the Abraham Manchester store in Adamsville, Rhode Island, in the 1800s catalogs some of the goods: "There were the spool chest; a cabinet for razor straps and another for carriage varnishes; special drawers for hunting caps, work gloves, blotting sand, bandannas, and clotheslines; the rack for horsewhips and ox gads"—or switches.

Abe's store is long gone, but Gray's, a competitor, is open today, as it has been for more than 200 years. Jimmy Gray "was a different kind of storekeeper," the same account says, "easy as to credit, always running out of things, taking a day off now and then to trade cows." The claim has been made that Gray's is the oldest continuously operating store in the United States.

Up the road from Gray's sits a stone gristmill, once as essential to the town as the store. The Massachusetts–Rhode Island line runs diagonally through the pond across the street from it. The miller, Tim McTague, is a lively Canadian who learned milling from John Hart, a third-generation Gray who owned the business for 62 years.

Hart had sold it to a New Yorker, Ralph Guild, who had promised to keep it running. "Ralph wanted to prevent it from becoming another boutique," Tim told me. "I was delighted when I heard they were looking for an apprentice at the mill. I thought I'd never get an opportunity like this one."

A carpenter by trade, Tim had skills that came in handy in restoring the mill. Instead of water, a 1946 Dodge—an old mayonnaise delivery truck—powers the wheel. Tim grinds the same strain of corn that was raised by the Narragansett Indians. It ages for nine months in open-air cribs, which hardens it for grinding.

As I watched, Tim poured yellow kernels into the hopper. "The top stone is the runner stone, and the bottom is the millstone," he said, lifting the screw jack that separates the two stones. "As the runner stone turns, grooves in the granite cut across each other. This pushes the grain to the outside edges." In moments the grain began falling onto a mesh screen below. "An old washing machine agitator powers it," Tim said. The screen sifts out some of the bran and the coarser kernels.

A woodcut of the mill, designed by Tim, marks the white bags that hold the ground corn and flour. "As far as I'm concerned," Tim mused as he measured flour onto a scale in the packaging room, "I have a great product here. It's pure, it has a nice rich flavor, there's no plastic in our packaging. Sure, the meal has a short shelf life, but it will keep for months in a refrigerator.

"I sell to stores, restaurants, and chefs in Boston, Philadelphia, and New York. And I have a good mail order business. But I think we probably would have better patronage if we were in a city." After a moment, he added, "I guess I had illusions

Sunlight patterns an aged window in the Old North Church in North Danville, Vermont. Only kerosene lanterns light its interior.

about how profitable the business would be. It's easier and cheaper for people simply to buy a bag of Pillsbury flour."

I asked him why he stays on at the mill. Again he paused, then said, "I guess I must enjoy it, because I'm certainly not making any money at it. I know it sounds crazy. But the mill is one of those wonderful old things that doesn't make sense, so why stop now? There's been a tradition of milling here since the 1700s. It would be sad to shut it down."

A similar philosophy motivates Howard Whitcomb. For four weekends each year he operates his turn-of-the-century cider press, preserving an autumn tradition that goes back centuries.

The Old Red Cider Mill sits alongside Maine Route 139 in Monroe. Howard's father, Orville, bought it in the 1960s; in 1978 he sold it to Howard, whose first task was to repair the roof, which had fallen in. According to local tradition, it is one of the oldest presses still operating in the state.

On the blustery morning I arrived, a fourth-generation customer had brought in several barrels of apples. Orville was picking stems and leaves off them, then shoving them into a grinder. With his white beard and rosy cheeks, he looked like Santa Claus. Below, Howard was squashing the pulp of the apples through layers of cloth with a wooden paddle.

"My father looks forward to this every year," Howard shouted above the clatter of the press. A complex system of pipes and tanks gathered the juice from the pulp, fed it through various stages, then siphoned it into plastic jugs. Howard knows his trade and a lot about apples. Russets and Cortlands make the best cider, he thinks.

"This isn't my regular job," Howard said. "I really do it just for fun." He stuffed another log into the stove in the next room; a dog there wagged its tail, as if happy to have found a warm spot on this chilly day. "Some of my regular customers live a hundred miles away," Howard said. "Schoolteachers, woodcutters, dentists. I think they like our cider because it takes them back a few years."

Nostalgia was a theme I had sensed all across the byways of New England. For some people maintaining a thread to the past means working with their hands or on the land; for others, like Howard, it means keeping alive time-honored skills and customs. Perhaps more than uncluttered space, rural New England is people—people who cherish the plain life-style and the basic values that are harder to hold on to in a city, people who are determined to keep alive their independence and individuality in a rapidly changing world.

"Yes," said Howard, as he cranked up the press again. "It kinda takes 'em back."

Outside, the season's first snow had begun to fall. White crystals speckled the dead leaves carpeting the ground. Autumn was waning, and as I hurried to my car I knew it was time to leave New England. The highways and byways would soon fill with snow; darkness would come in the afternoons and linger in the mornings; and the pace of life would slow nearly to a stop. I recalled something a Vermont farmer had said: "When the snow comes, what isn't done, doesn't get done."

Autumn moon rises over the distant White Mountains. Tiny Peacham nestles in Vermont's remote

Northeast Kingdom—a region of dense forests and lakes now being changed by increasing development.

Lyndon Institute meets Montpelier High for a game in Lyndonville, Vermont. Surrounding towns use the Institute as their high school. At left, Hagerty children arrive home from their regional school in South Hiram, Maine. Older facilities serve in Granby, Vermont (right): One teacher teaches eight students in a one-room schoolhouse.

Small-town events offer big-time pleasures: A once-a-year chicken potpie dinner draws a crowd to the town hall in Sheffield, Vermont. A few miles away in Danville, villagers gather for a summer band concert (lower left). In Dummerston Center's Congregational Church (below), 1,500 pies line pews during the annual Apple Pie Festival.

"I see my work, in part, as a way to preserve the old ways and designs," says Vermont quilter Merial Liberty. Here she stitches a patriotic pattern of her own design. George "Dutch" Kayser (above), of North Waterford, Maine, keeps alive another art: wheelwrighting, which he learned from his father. Vermont's Curtis Tuff (below) turns out tempting pork barbecue from a converted school bus.

Farm cat's paradise: barns, barns, barns. This Vermont dairy farmer's fascination with the structures

is a fitting one: New England's well-tended barns survive in beautiful profusion.

Handler Ricky Thompson and his friend April Audette check out the competition during a horse pulling event at the Lamoille County Field Days in Johnson, Vermont. Dexter and Dan seem unconcerned. They went on to place second; the first-place team managed to pull the contest's whopping 10,000-pound load a few inches farther. Another first-place winner was the ewe (above) shown by 4-H'er Michelle Walker at a fair in Barre, Massachusetts.

Morning and evening, Marilyn Magnus tends her flock near Peacham, Vermont. From the animals' fleece she spins yarn, which she then weaves into rugs. A more seasonal task occupies workers (above) in Plymouth, Massachusetts; with wooden scrubbers they corral cranberries in a bog flooded for harvest. A worker at Presque Isle, Maine, (below) inspects freshly dug potatoes headed for storage.

"I have seen no village more beautiful," said Washington Irving of Orford, New Hampshire. Here

autumn storm clouds gather above the Wheeler House, one of several historic homes in the hamlet.

Nose to nose, 18-month-old Patrick Russ greets Andy, his family's prizewinning entry in the Barre fair. For 25 years the fair has offered a showcase for the work and hobbies of young and old; some 1,200 attend the event, held each year on the last Sunday in July. Attractions include arts and crafts exhibits, livestock shows, and a frog-jumping contest.

A white church, a covered bridge, the flag, autumn leaves, pumpkins—the hallmarks of scenic New

England here crowd the banks of the Upper Ammonoosuc River in New Hampshire.

INDEX

Boldface indicates illustrations

Winding New England back road finds a farm—quiet on a sunny autumn morning—near Woodstock, Vermont.

DAVID F. HUGHES / THE PICTURE CUBE, BOSTON

Composition by the Typographic section of National Geographic Production Services, Pre-Press Division. Printed and bound by R. R. Donnelley & Sons, Willard, Ohio. Color separations by Graphic Art Service, Inc., Nashville, Tenn.; Lanman Progressive Company, Washington, D. C.; and Lincoln Graphics, Inc., Cherry Hill, N.J. Dust jacket printed by Federated Lithographers-Printers, Inc., Providence, R.I.

Library of Congress ℂℙ Data
New England, land of scenic splendor.
  Bibliography: p.
  Includes index.
  1. New England—
Description and travel—1981- 2.
New England—Description and travel—1981- —Views I. National Geographic Society (U.S.). Special Publications Division.
F10.N48 1989   974   89-12127
ISBN 0-87044-715-7
ISBN 0-87044-720-3 (lib. ed.)

Notes on Contributors

A free-lance photographer, Nicholas DeVore III has handled assignments for the National Geographic Society for 17 years. In Colorado, where he lives, he helped establish Photographers/Aspen, a photo syndicate, and is a member of the board of the Aspen Art Museum.

Fluent in five languages, free-lance writer/photographer Tor Eigeland first contributed to National Geographic in 1966 with "Capturing Strange Creatures in Colombia." Recent work includes an article on the fjords of his native Norway for National Geographic Traveler.

With the Society since 1974, staff writer Christine Eckstrom Lee holds a degree in English from Mount Holyoke College in Massachusetts. She previously reported on the Northeast in the Special Publication *Window on America* and on the East Coast in *America's Atlantic Isles.*

A graduate of the University of Missouri School of Journalism, free-lance photographer Sarah Leen covered Uganda as an intern with the National Geographic Society in 1979. Photographing the history of New England was her third assignment for Special Publications.

Jane R. McCauley lived in Geneva, Switzerland, for three years before joining the Society's staff in 1970. She has contributed to several Special Publications and has written eight books for children, including *Let's Explore A River* and the action book *Animals Showing Off.*

A native New Yorker and a graduate of Syracuse University, free-lance photographer Michael Melford has had his work appear in numerous publications—among them *Life, Geo,* and *Travel & Leisure.* Covering rural New England was his first assignment for the Society.

Tom Melham has spanned the globe as a staff writer for the Society, traveling south to Antarctica and north to the Arctic. His Special Publication *John Muir's Wild America* was published in 1976. A 1989 assignment will take him into the Amazon rain forest for *The Emerald Realm.*

Staff writer Cynthia Russ Ramsay has written for more than 20 Special Publications, traveling on assignment throughout the United States and to such foreign locales as Bali and Bhutan. She also served as managing editor for a series of books for children.

Not in Kansas anymore, free-lance photographer Phil Schermeister once worked for the Topeka *Capital-Journal* but now calls San Francisco home. He recently returned to the Midwest to photograph it for the Geographic's Special Publication *Window on America.*

Acknowledgments

The Special Publications Division is grateful to the individuals, agencies, and organizations named or quoted in this book, and to those cited here, for their cooperation and help during its preparation: Leonard Brooks, Charlie Chiodo, Ralph J. Crandall, Chuck Dunn, Robert P. Emlen, Louis Fazzano, Mel Kaplan, Robert Gilka, George and Jennifer Lodge, Sandra G. Lucas, Paul and Gwill Maeder, Maxwell Maize, Jeannette Neptune, Joseph A. Nicholas, Rick Paradis, Annabelle Robbins, Gary Roberts, Janet Serra, George B. Thomas, William A. Truslow, and Ian Worley.

Additional Reading

Readers may wish to consult the *National Geographic Index*, as well as National Geographic Traveler, for related books and articles. The following may also prove useful: The WPA American Guide Series; Edward Deming Andrews, *The People Called Shakers;* Ray Bearse, ed., *Maine: A Guide to the Vacation State;* Bill Caldwell, *Islands of Maine: Where America Really Began;* John W. Hakola, *Legacy of a Lifetime: The Story of Baxter State Park;* Nancy Hale, *New England Discovery;* John Harris, *Historic Walks in Old Boston;* Jay Itzkowitz, ed., *Insight Guide: New England;* Henry W. Longfellow, *The Poetical Works of Longfellow;* John McPhee, *The Survival of the Bark Canoe;* Samuel Eliot Morison, *The Maritime History of Massachusetts;* Vernon Nahrgang, ed., *Fodor's 89 New England;* Neal R. Peirce, *The New England States, People, Politics, and Power;* William S. Simmons, *Spirit of the New England Tribes;* Henry D. Thoreau, *The Maine Woods* and *Walden;* Christina Tree, *Maine: An Explorer's Guide;* Christina Tree and Peter Jennison, *Vermont: An Explorer's Guide;* Walter Muir Whitehill, *Boston, a Topographical History;* and David Yeadon, *Hidden Corners of New England.*